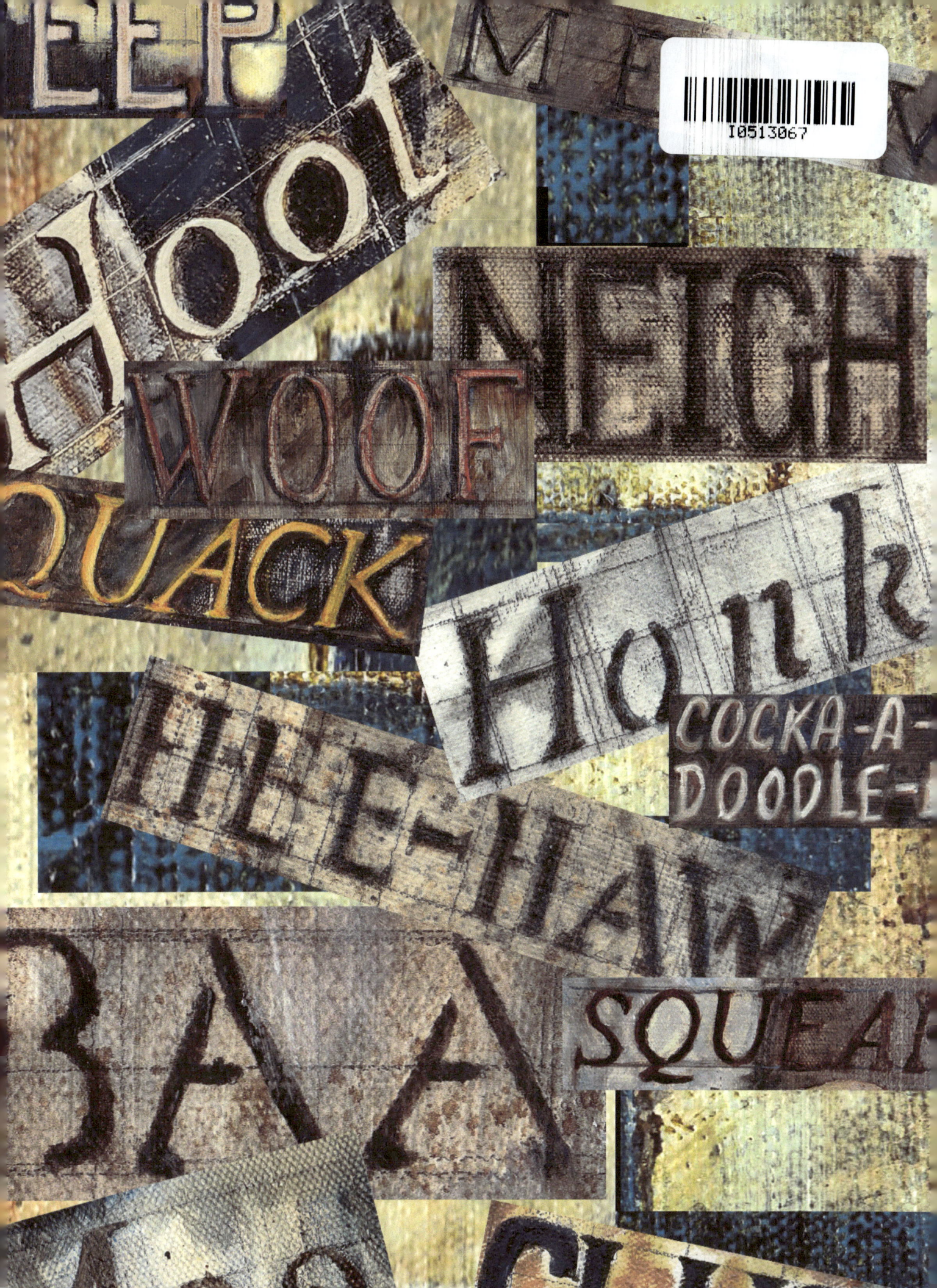

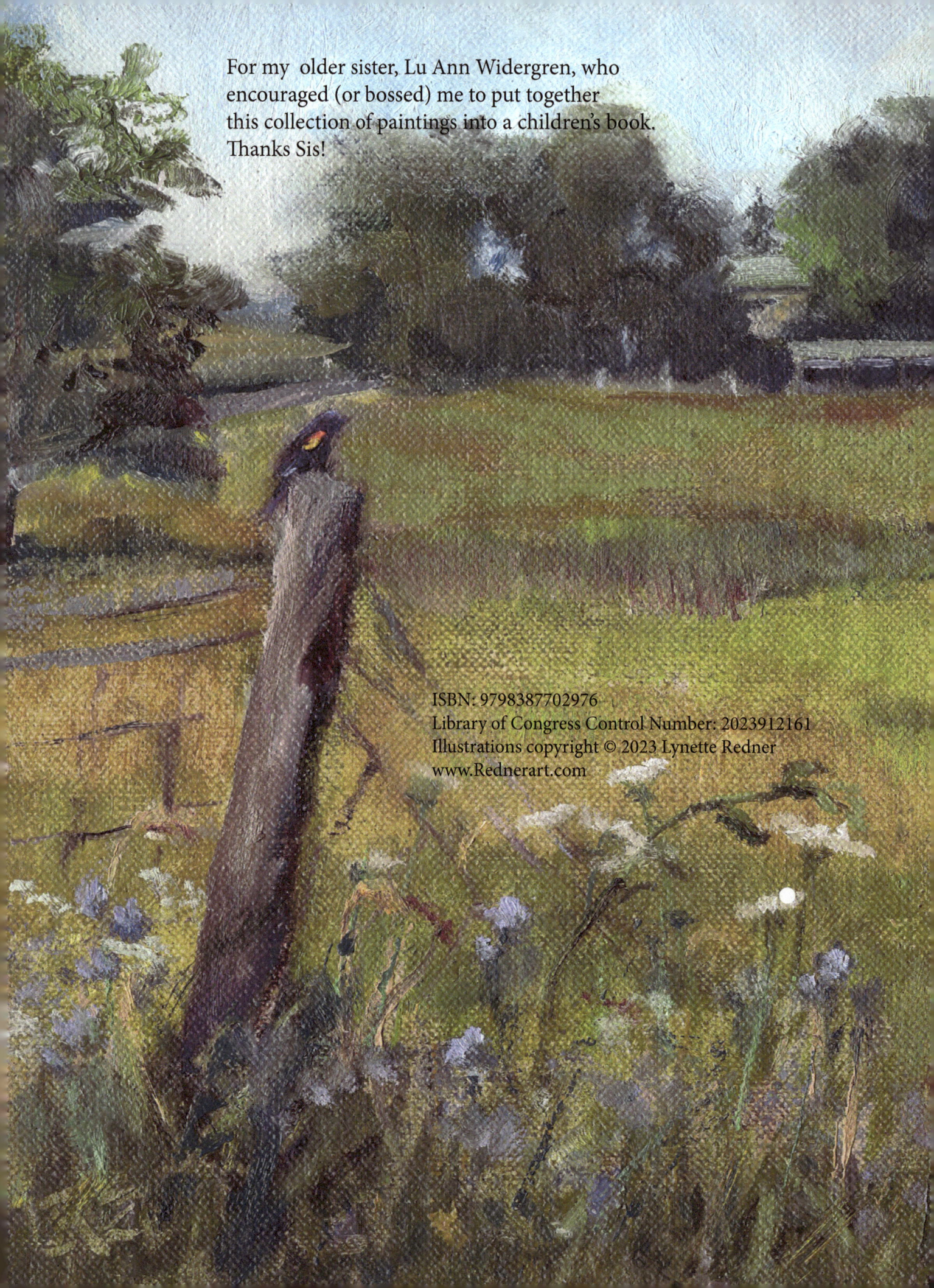

For my older sister, Lu Ann Widergren, who encouraged (or bossed) me to put together this collection of paintings into a children's book. Thanks Sis!

ISBN: 9798387702976
Library of Congress Control Number: 2023912161
Illustrations copyright © 2023 Lynette Redner
www.Rednerart.com

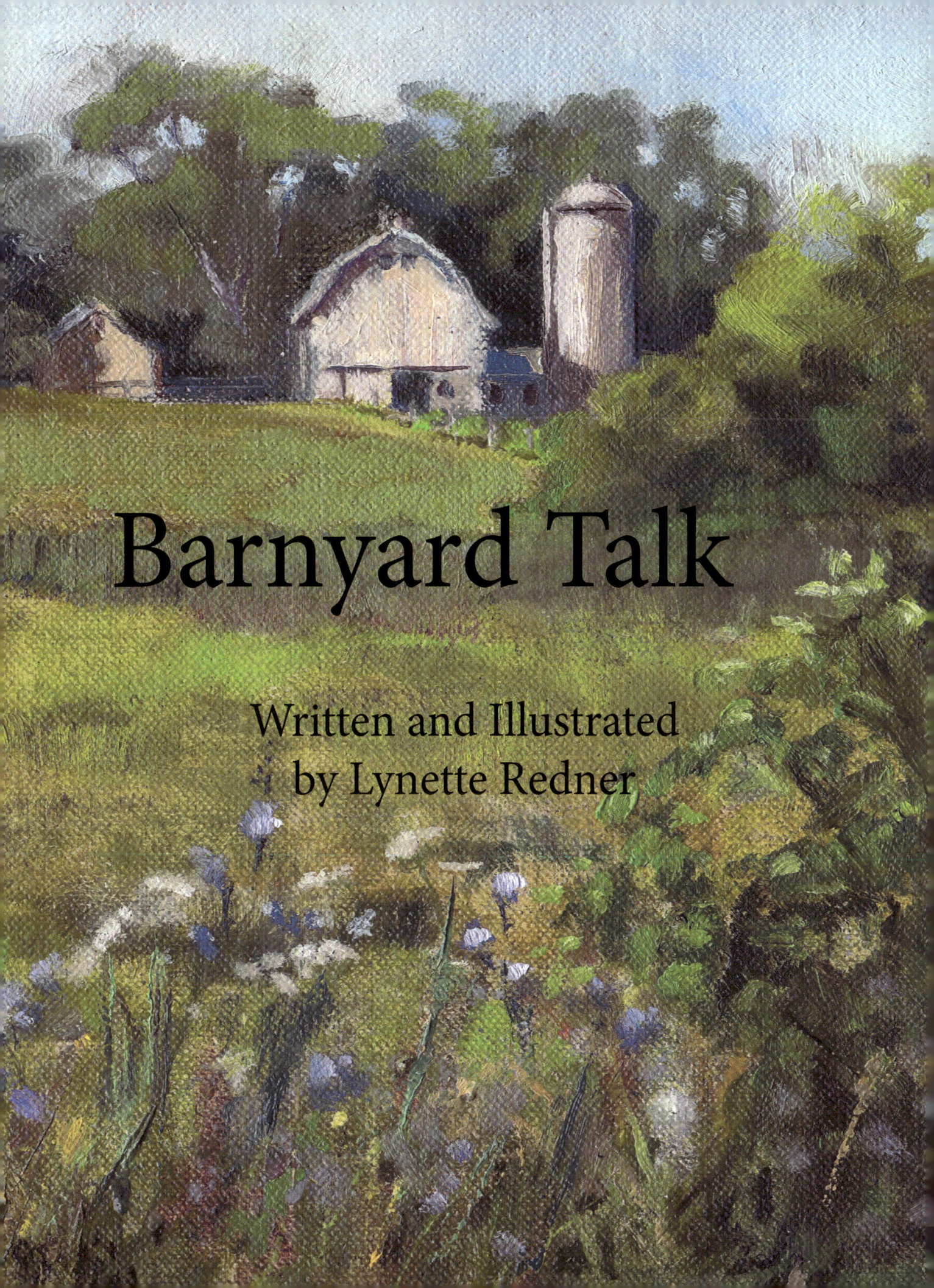

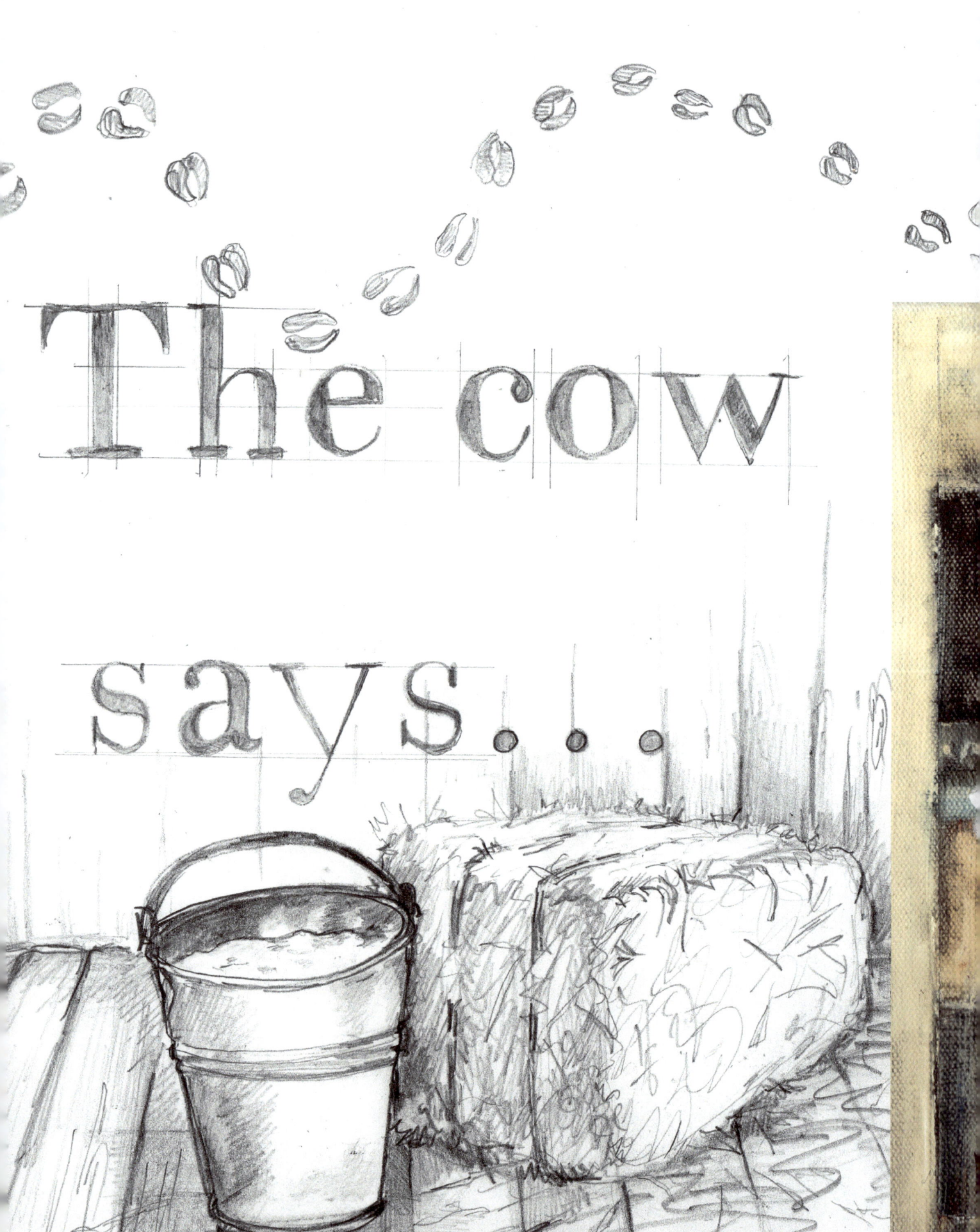

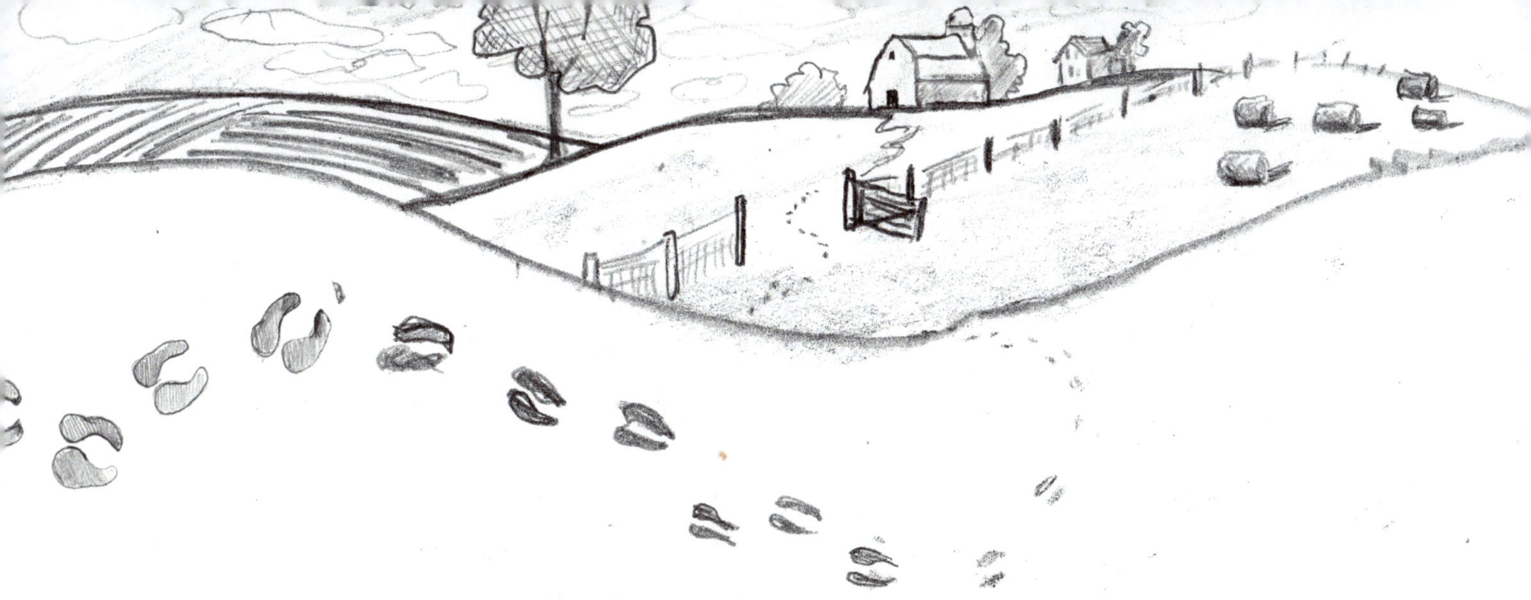

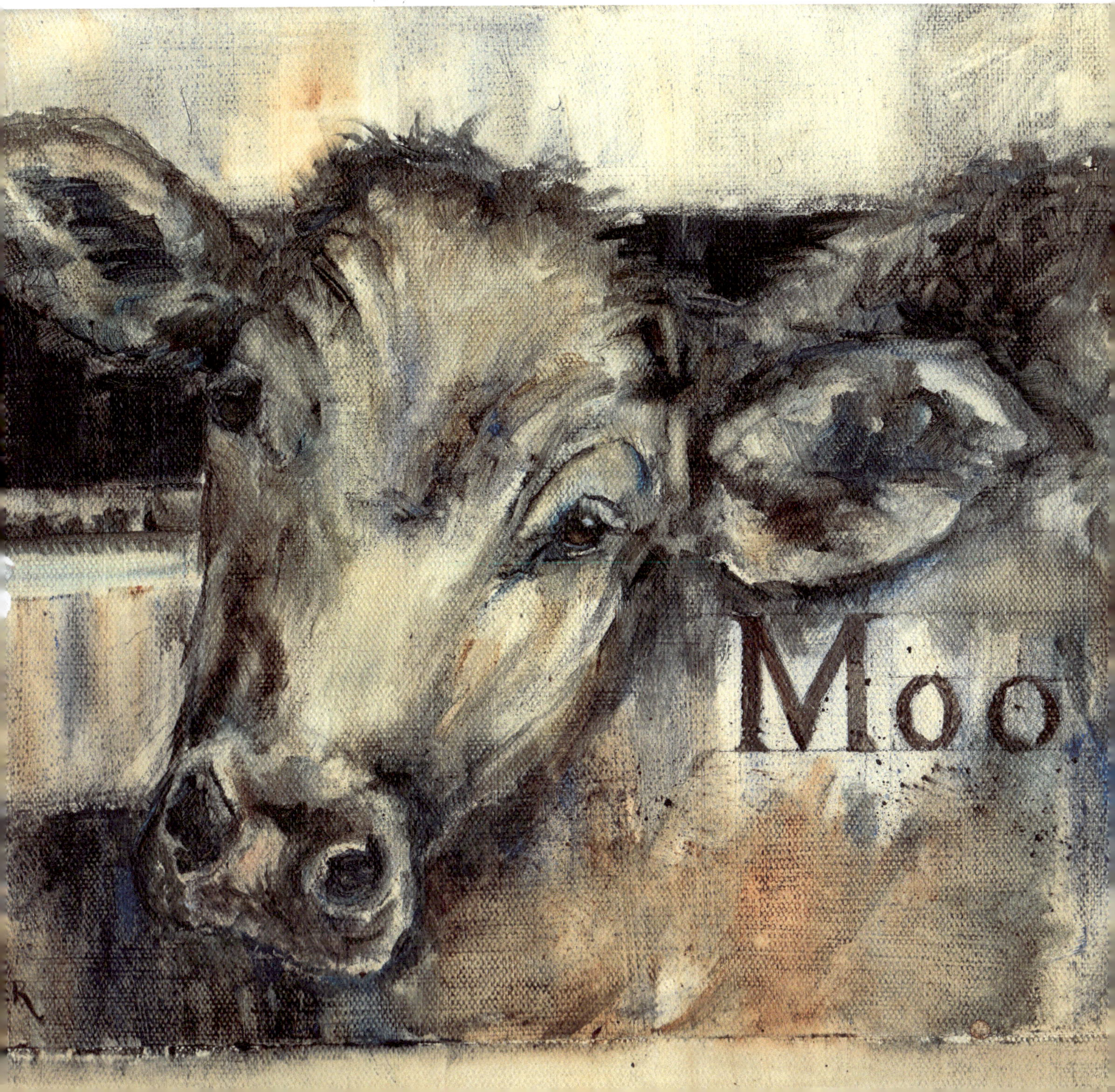

Moo

The little chicks go...

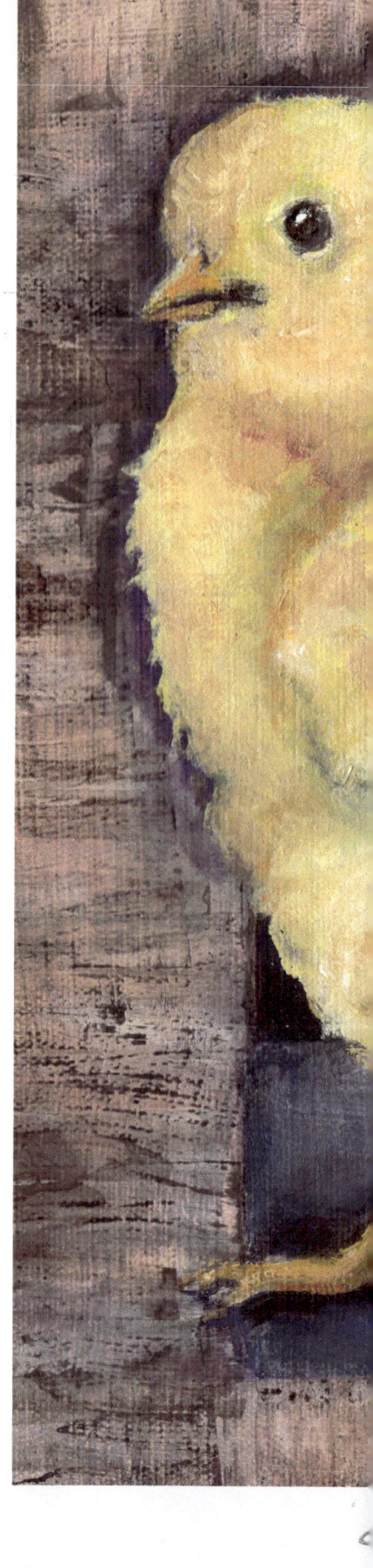
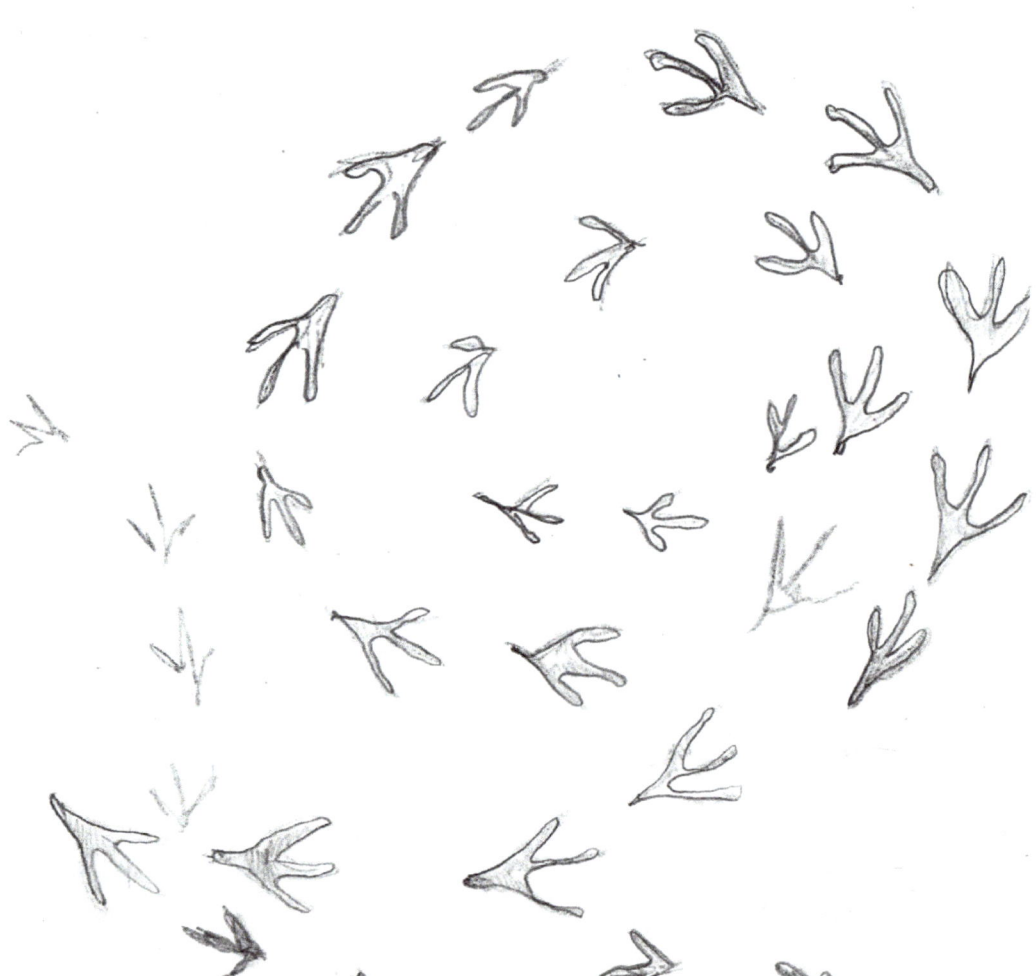

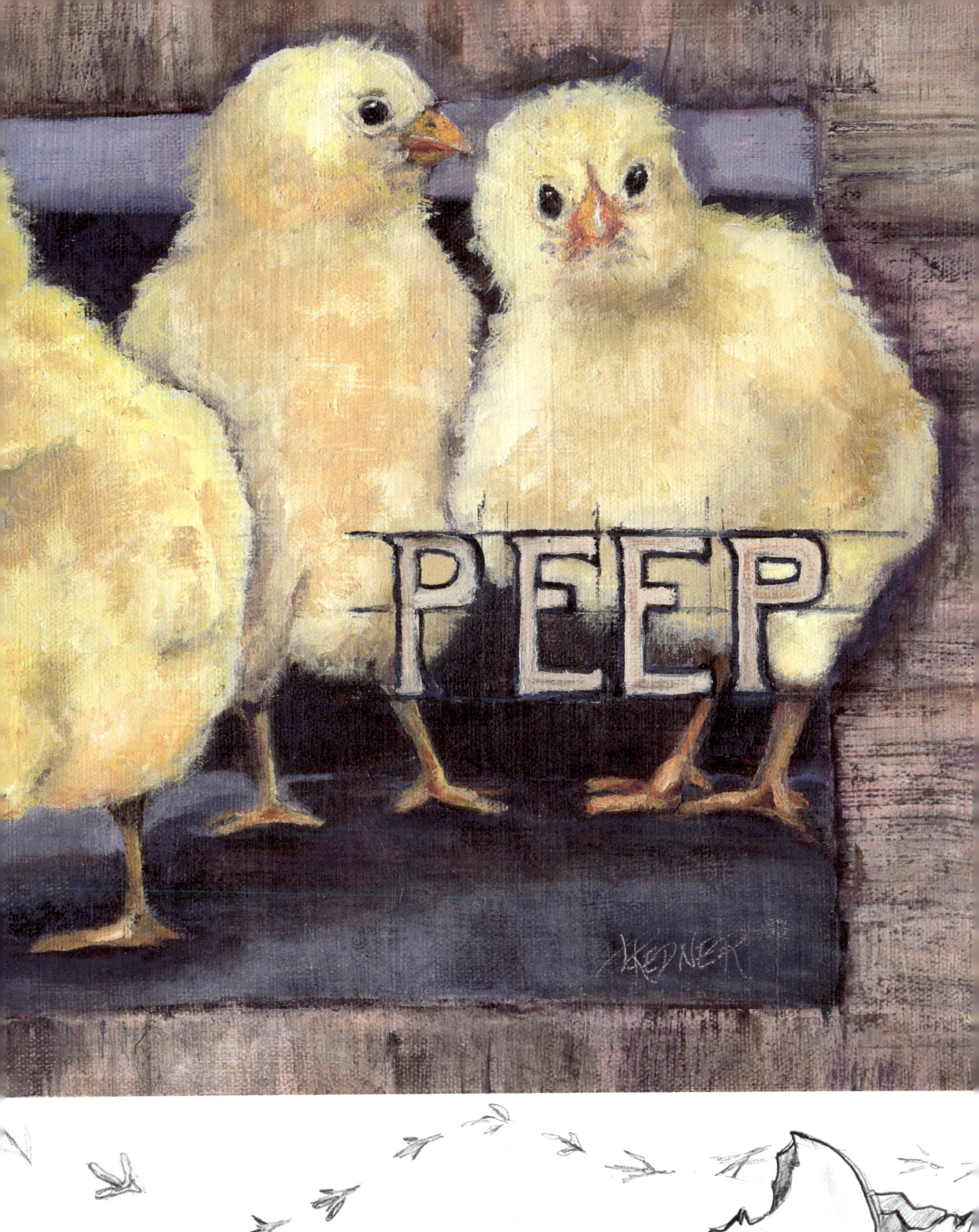

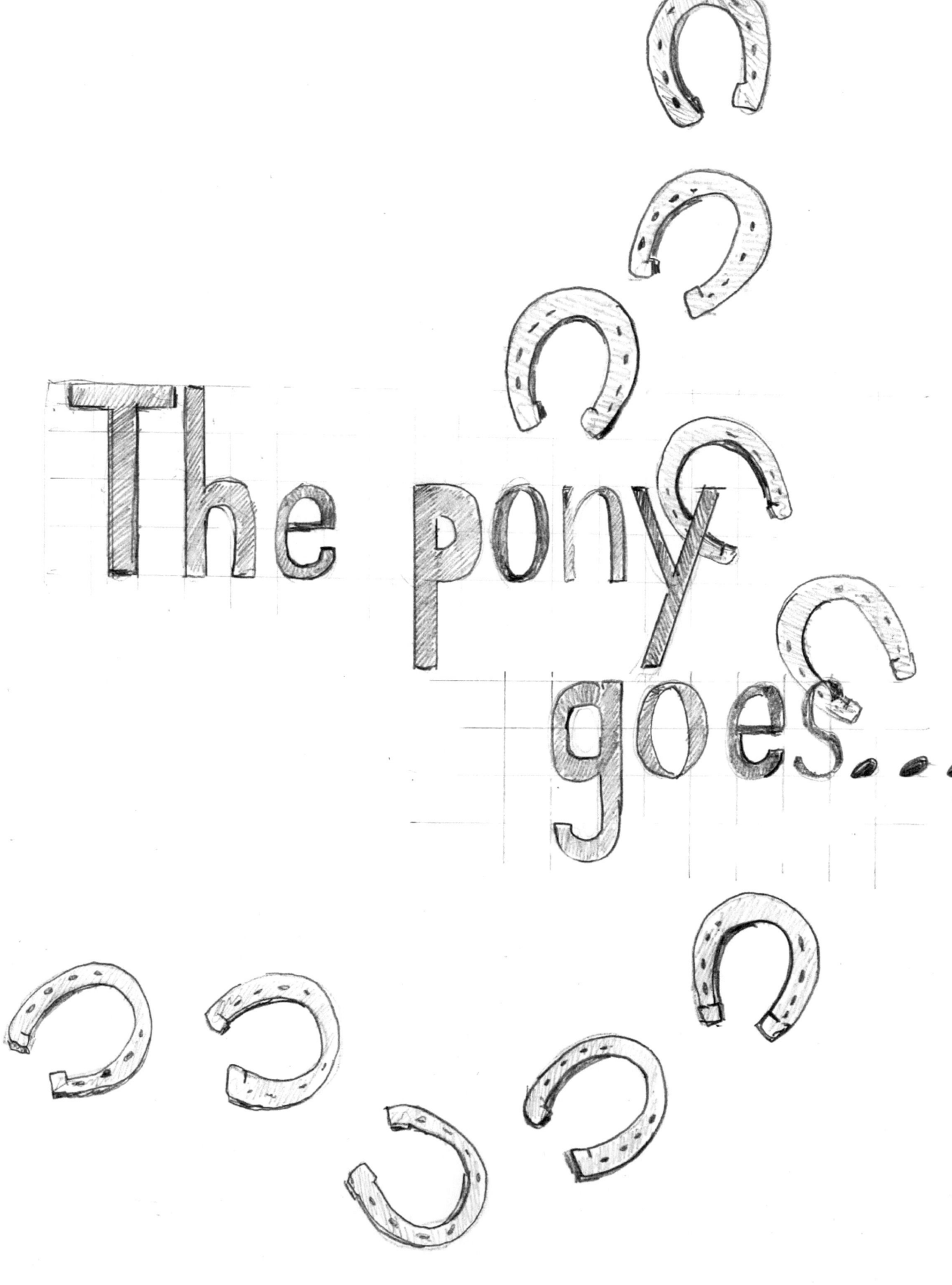

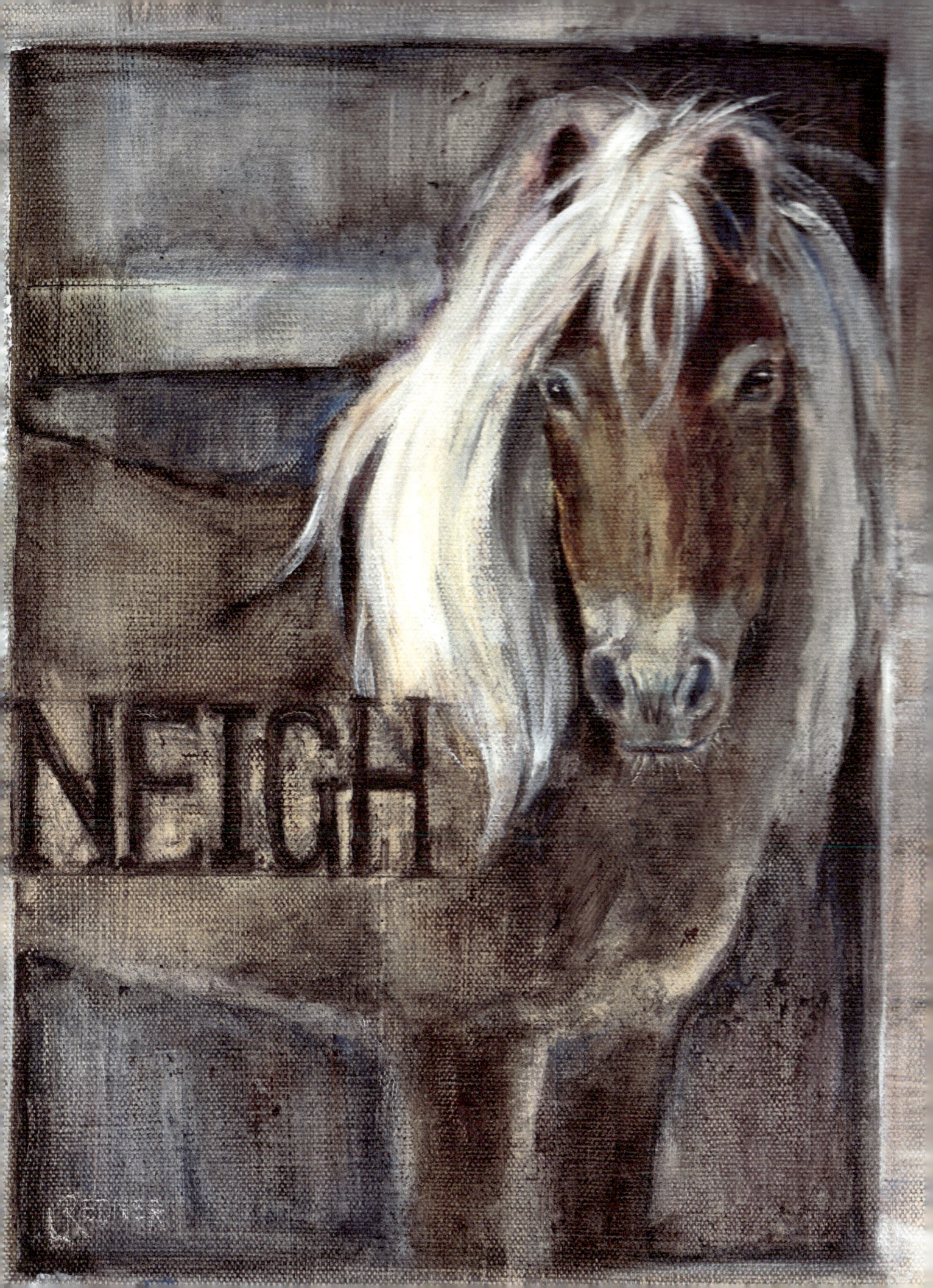

The duck goes....

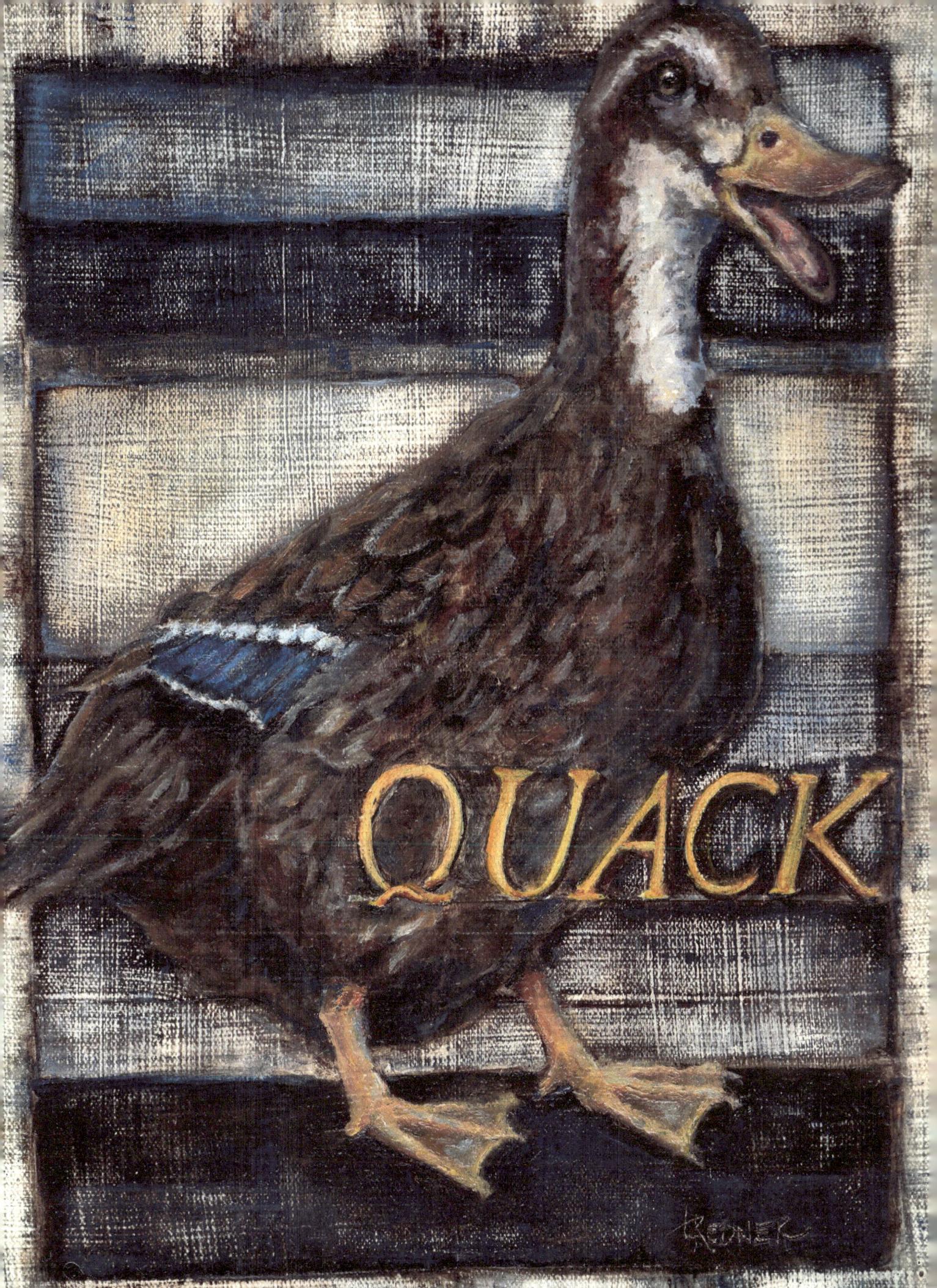

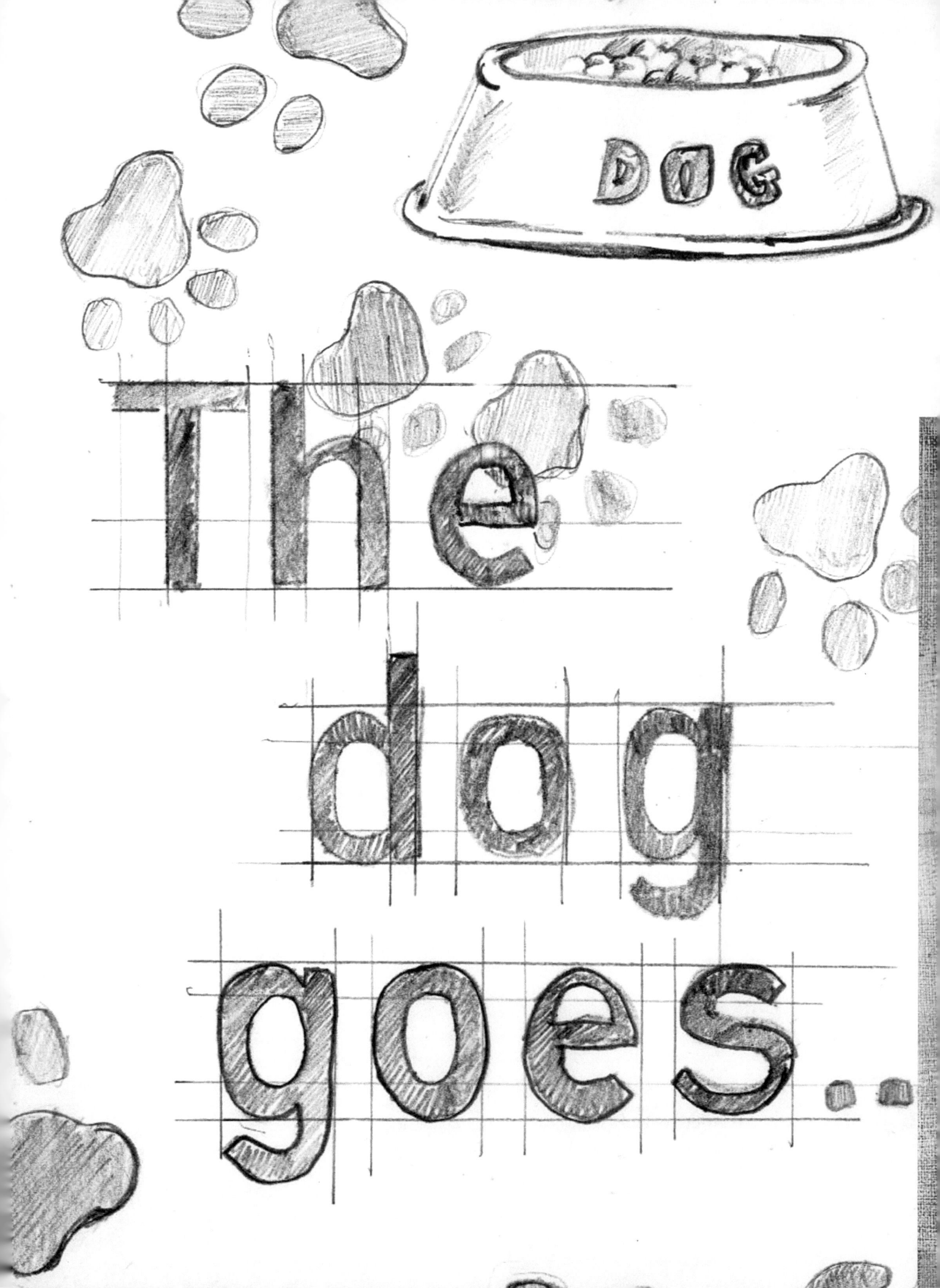

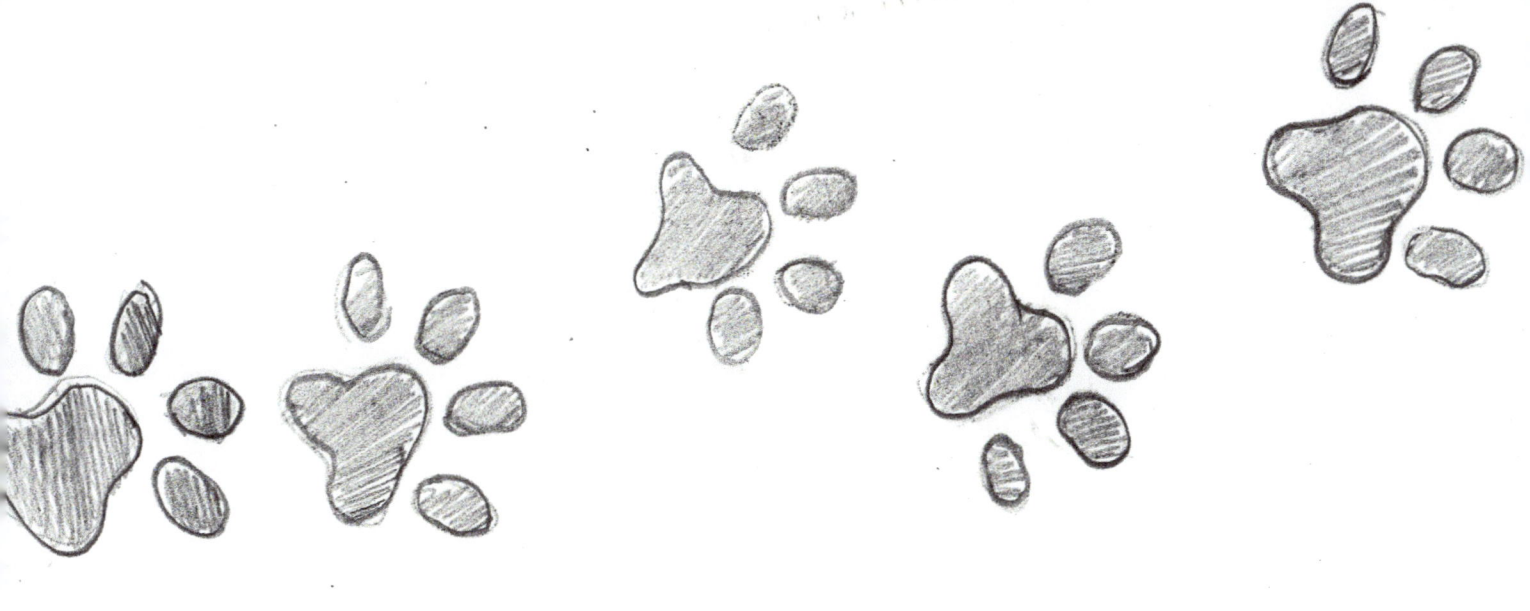

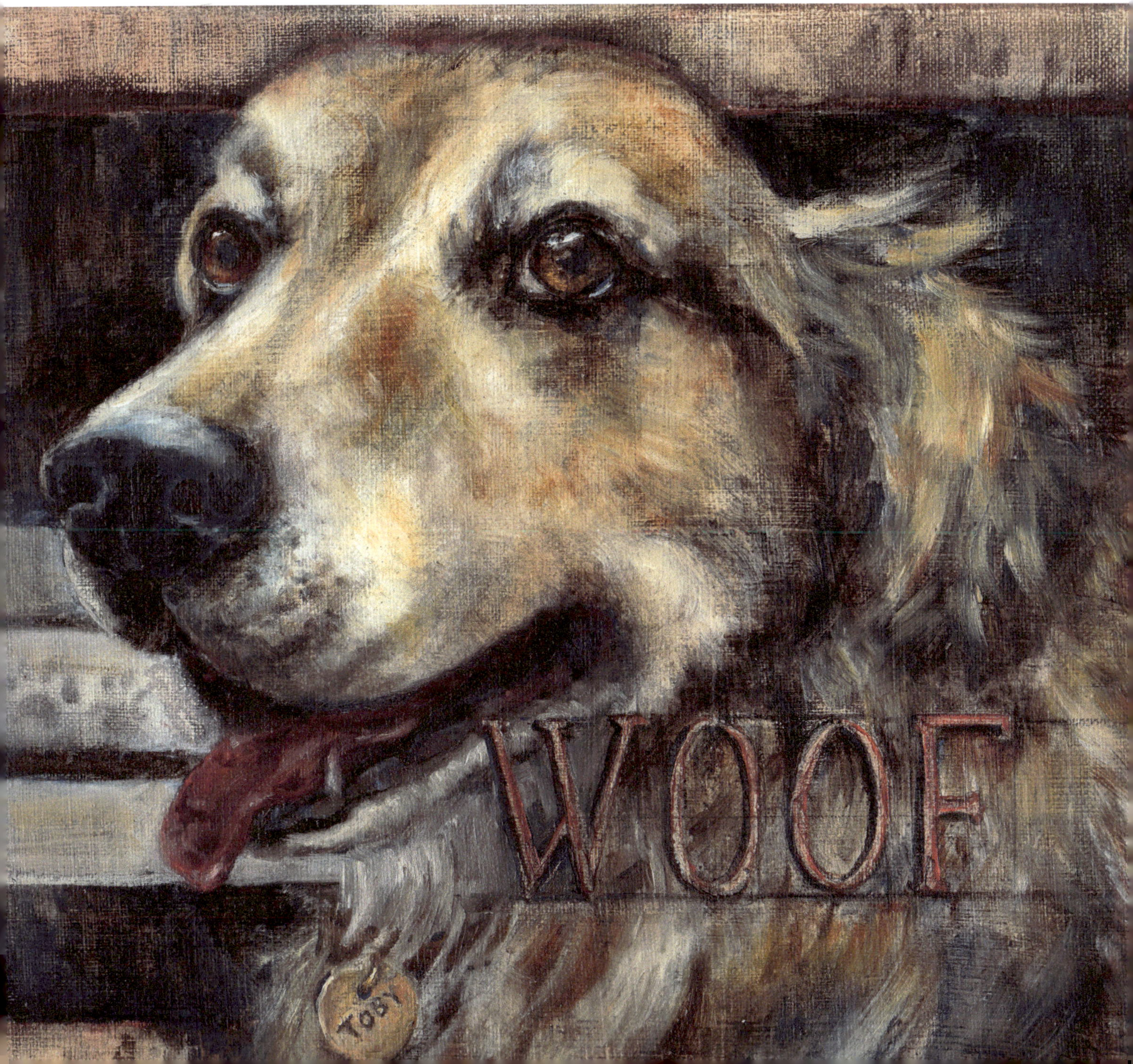

The cat purrs...

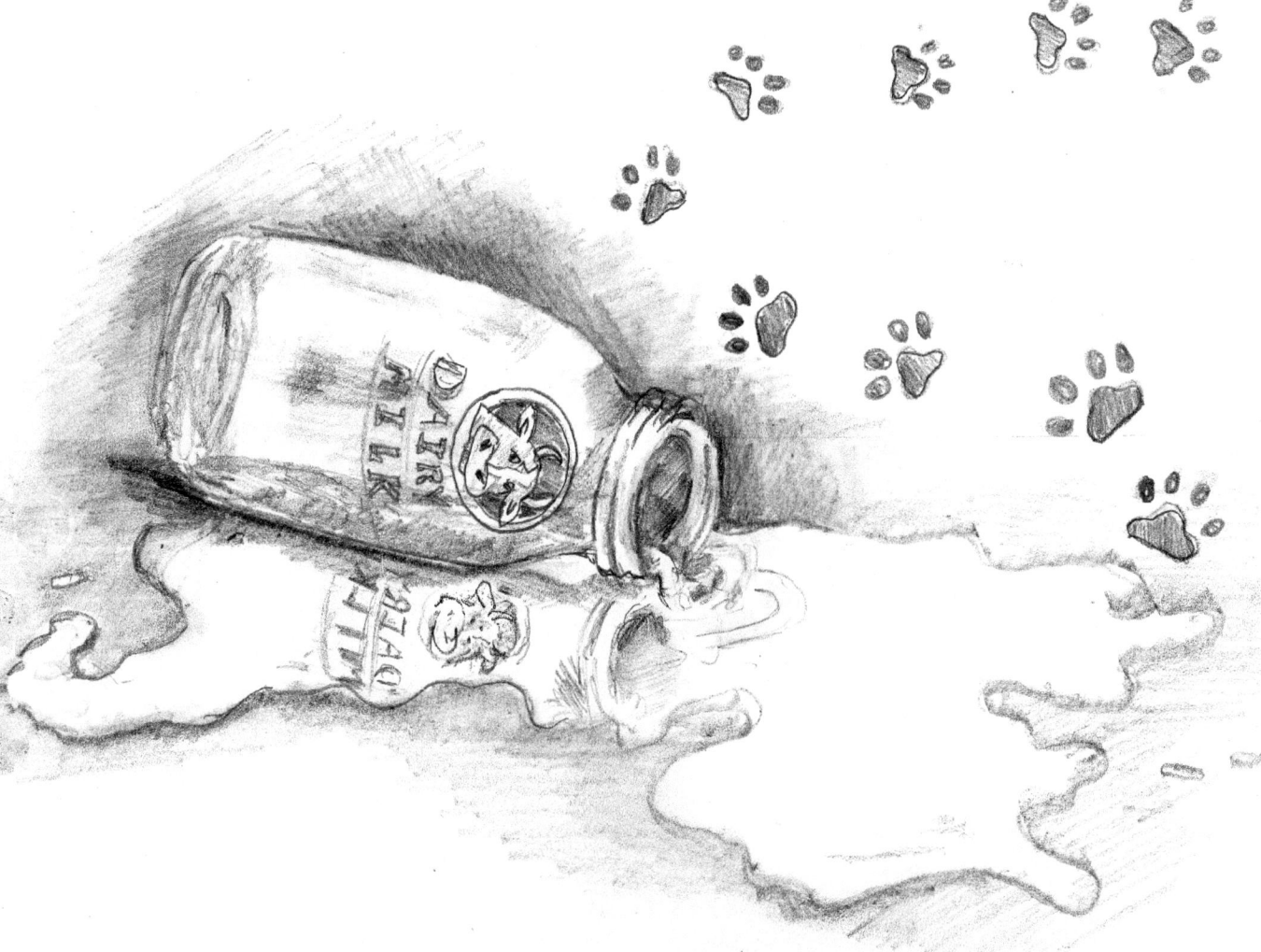

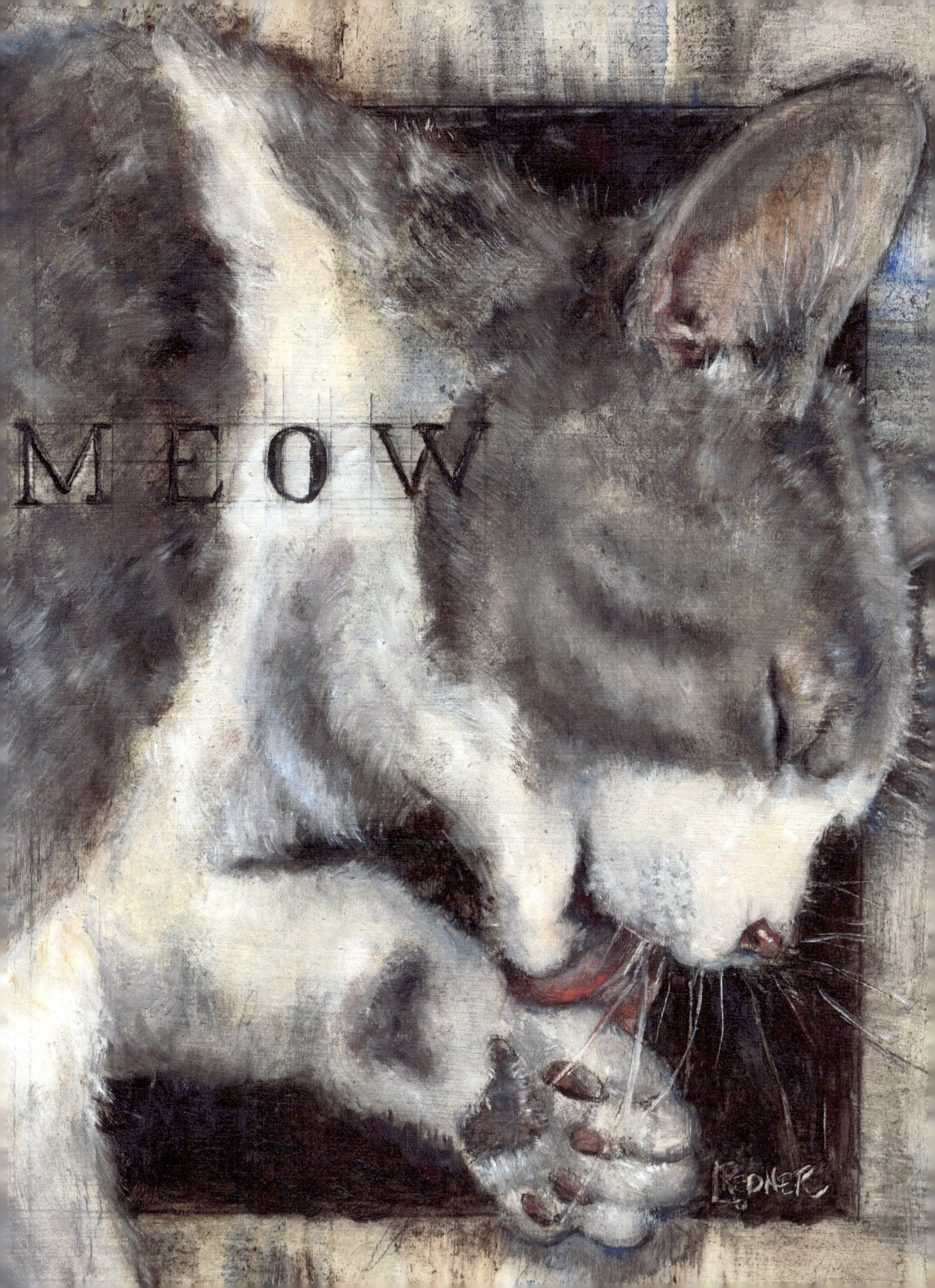

The mouse makes a...

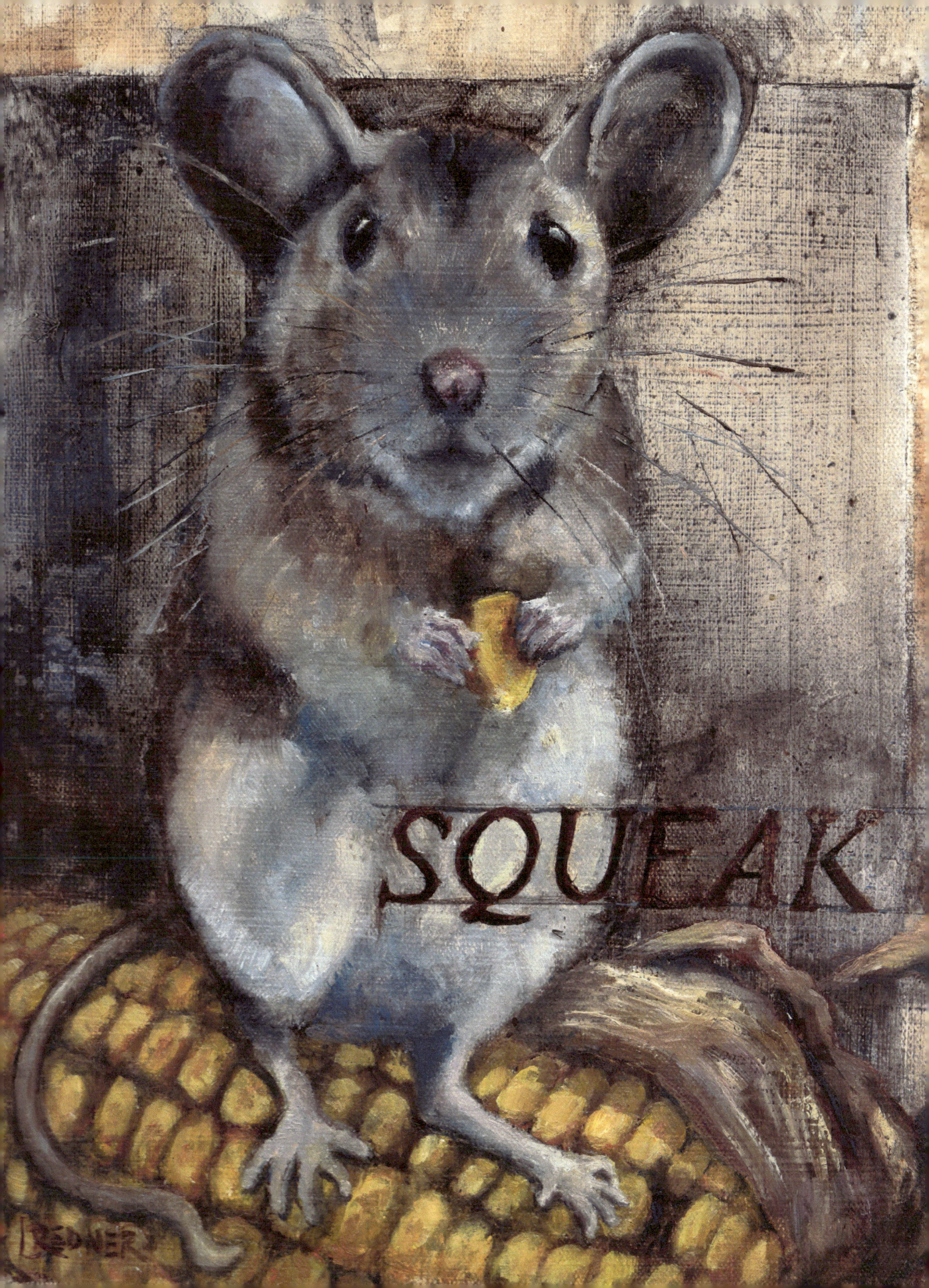

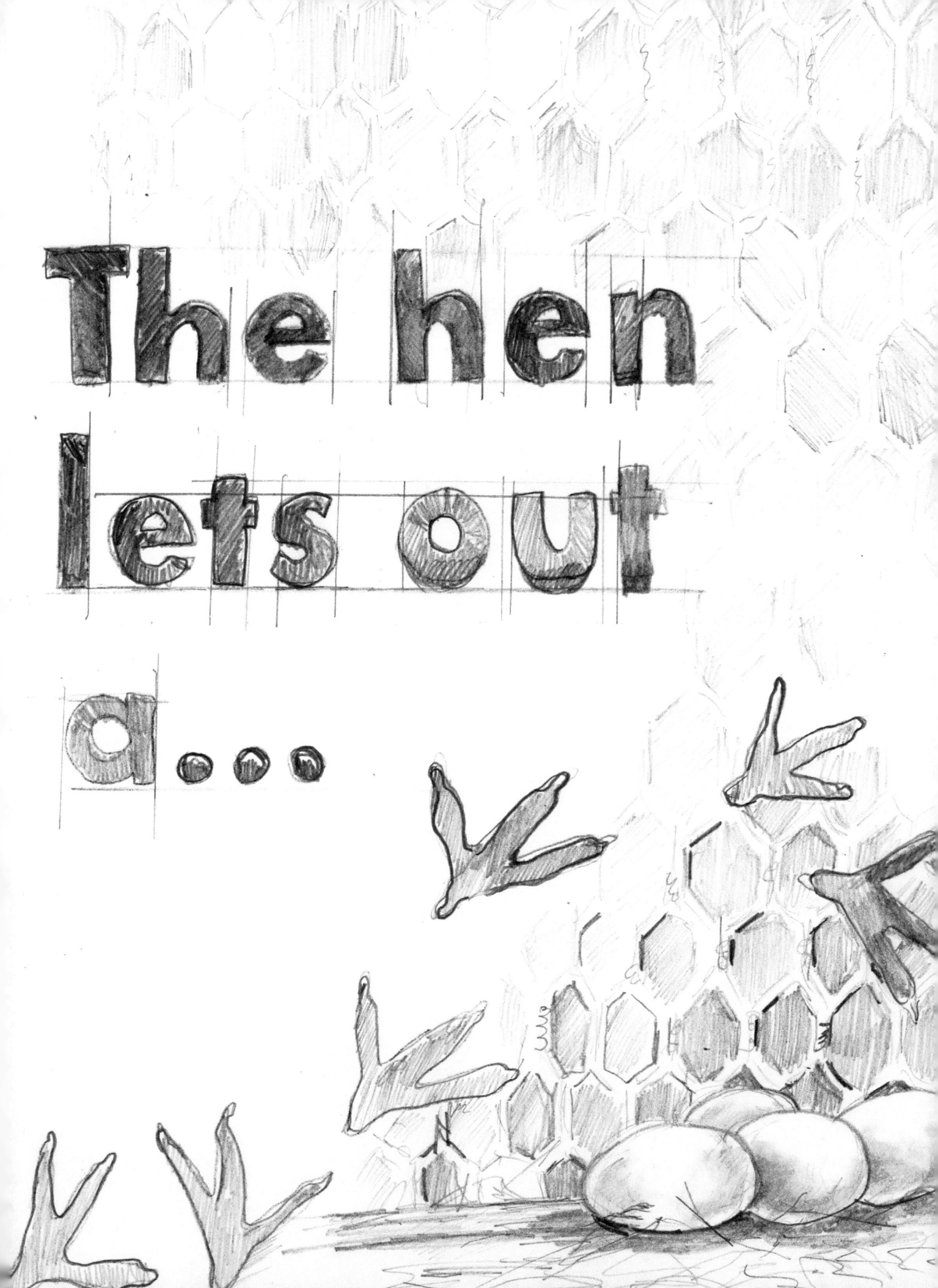

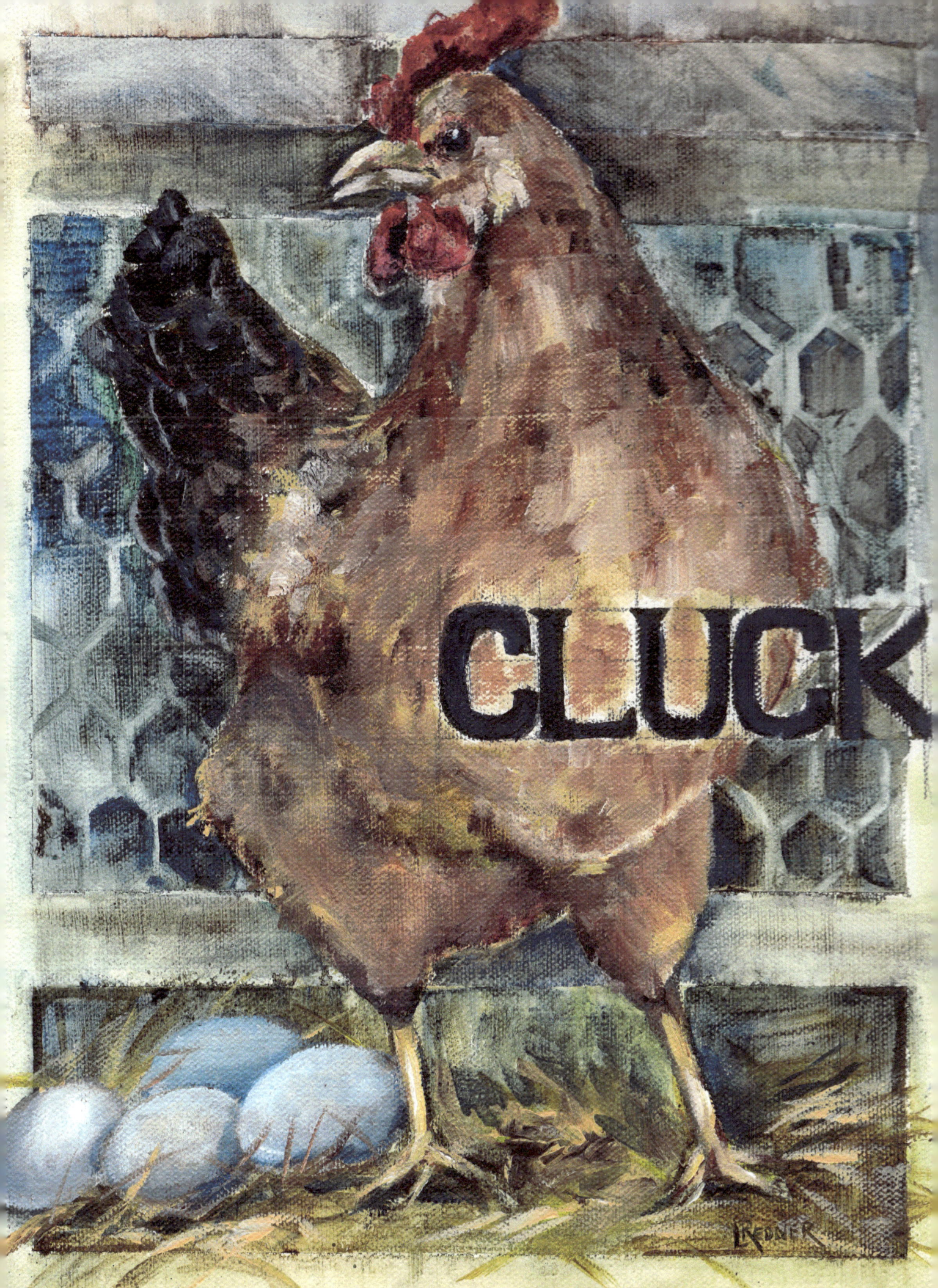

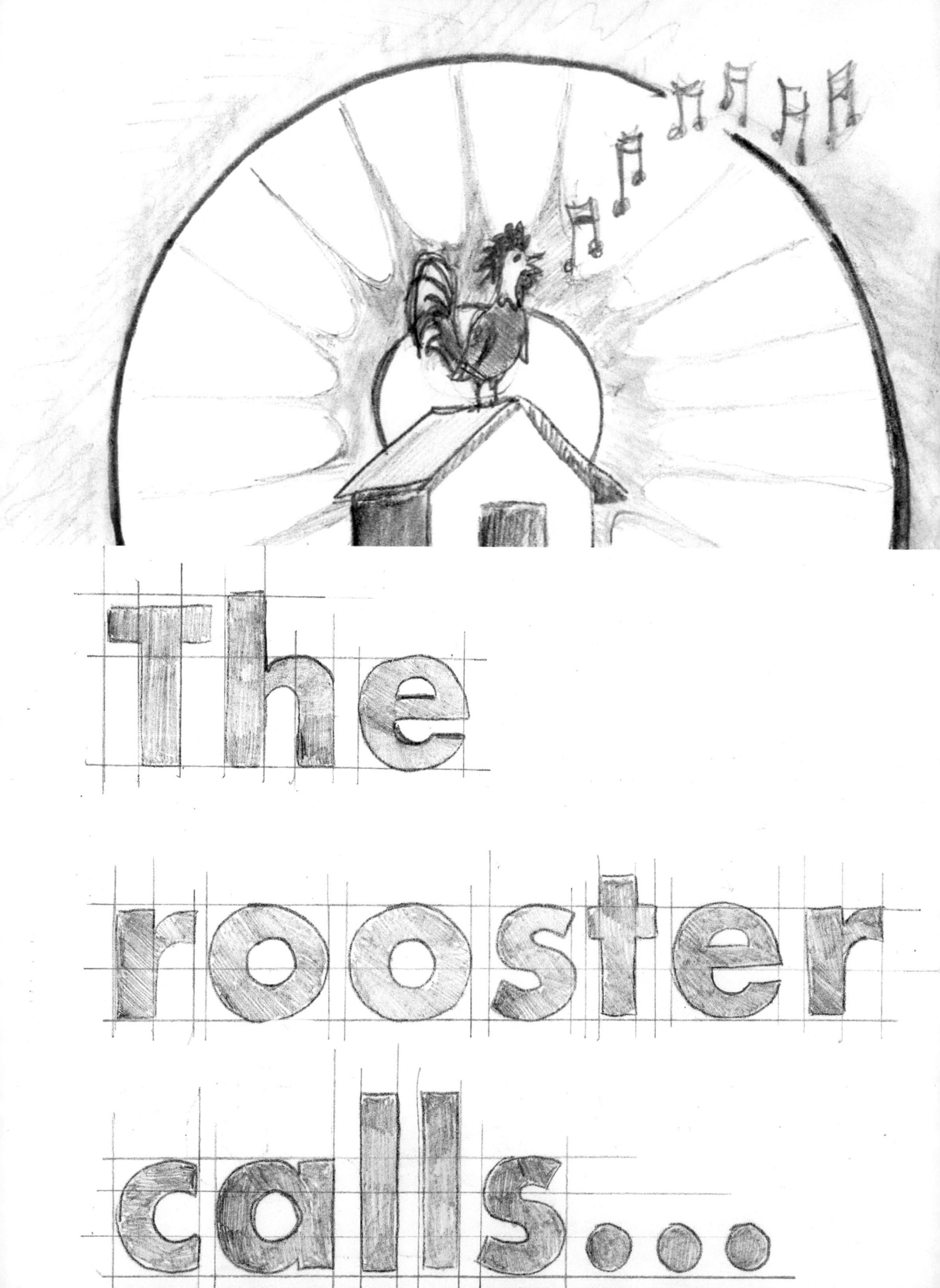

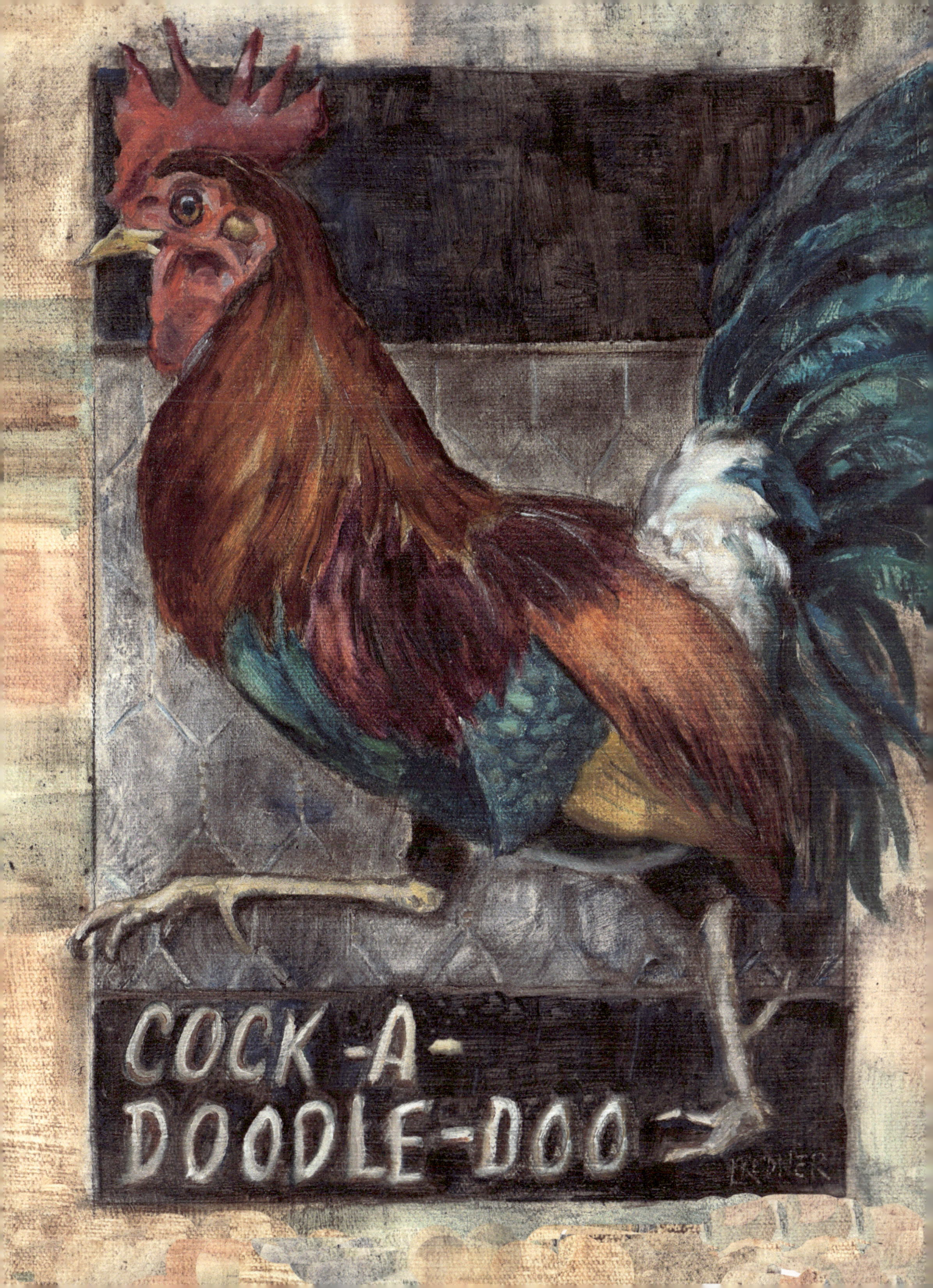

The pig goes...

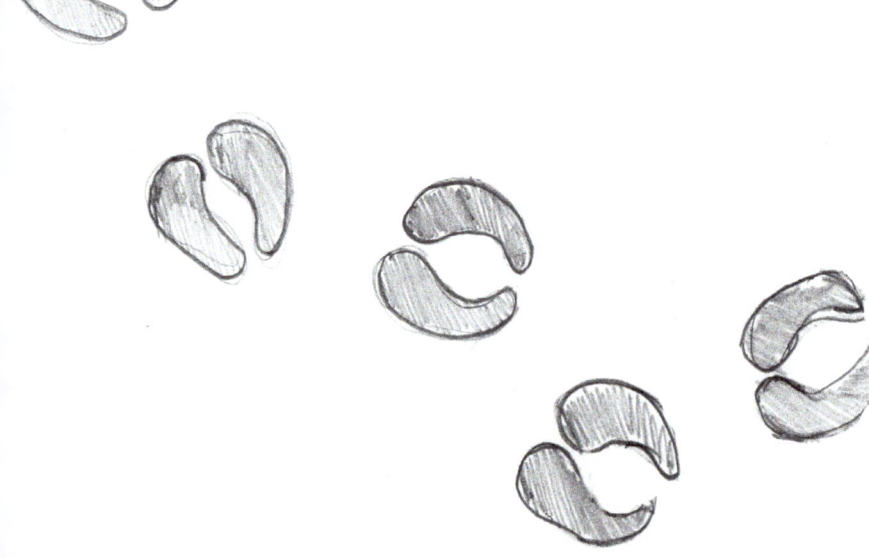
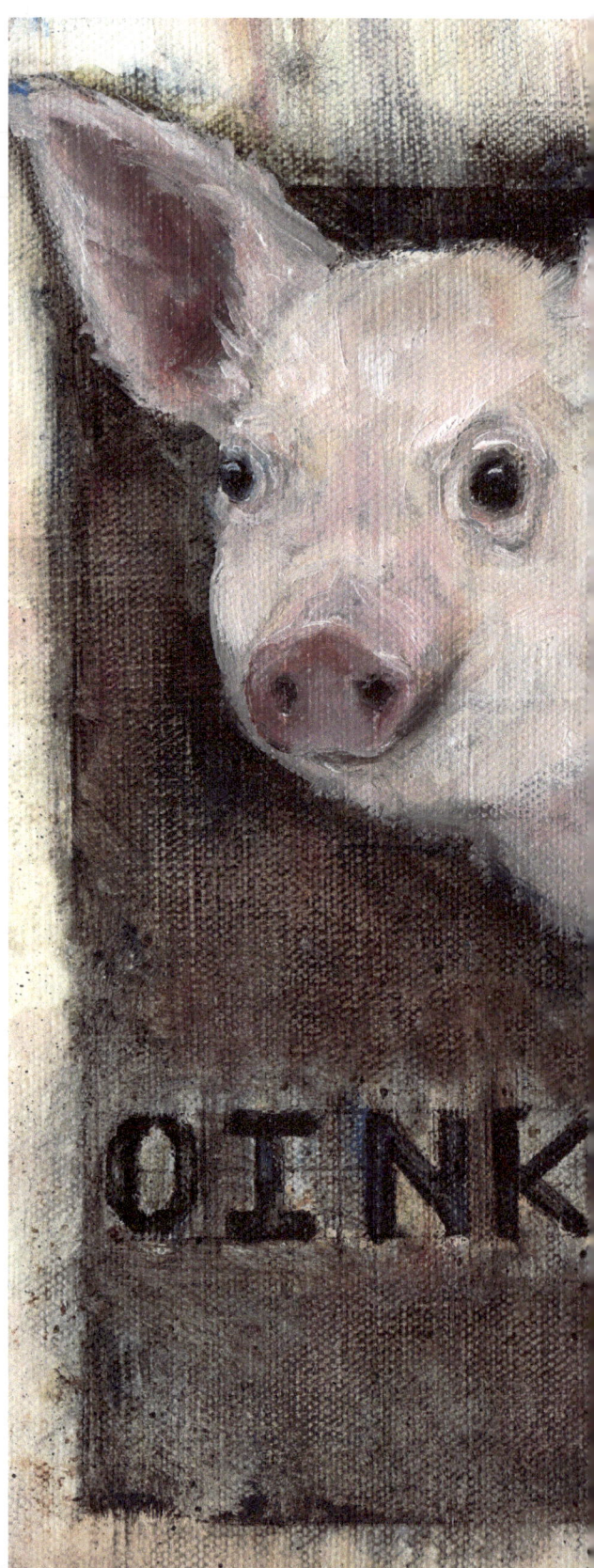

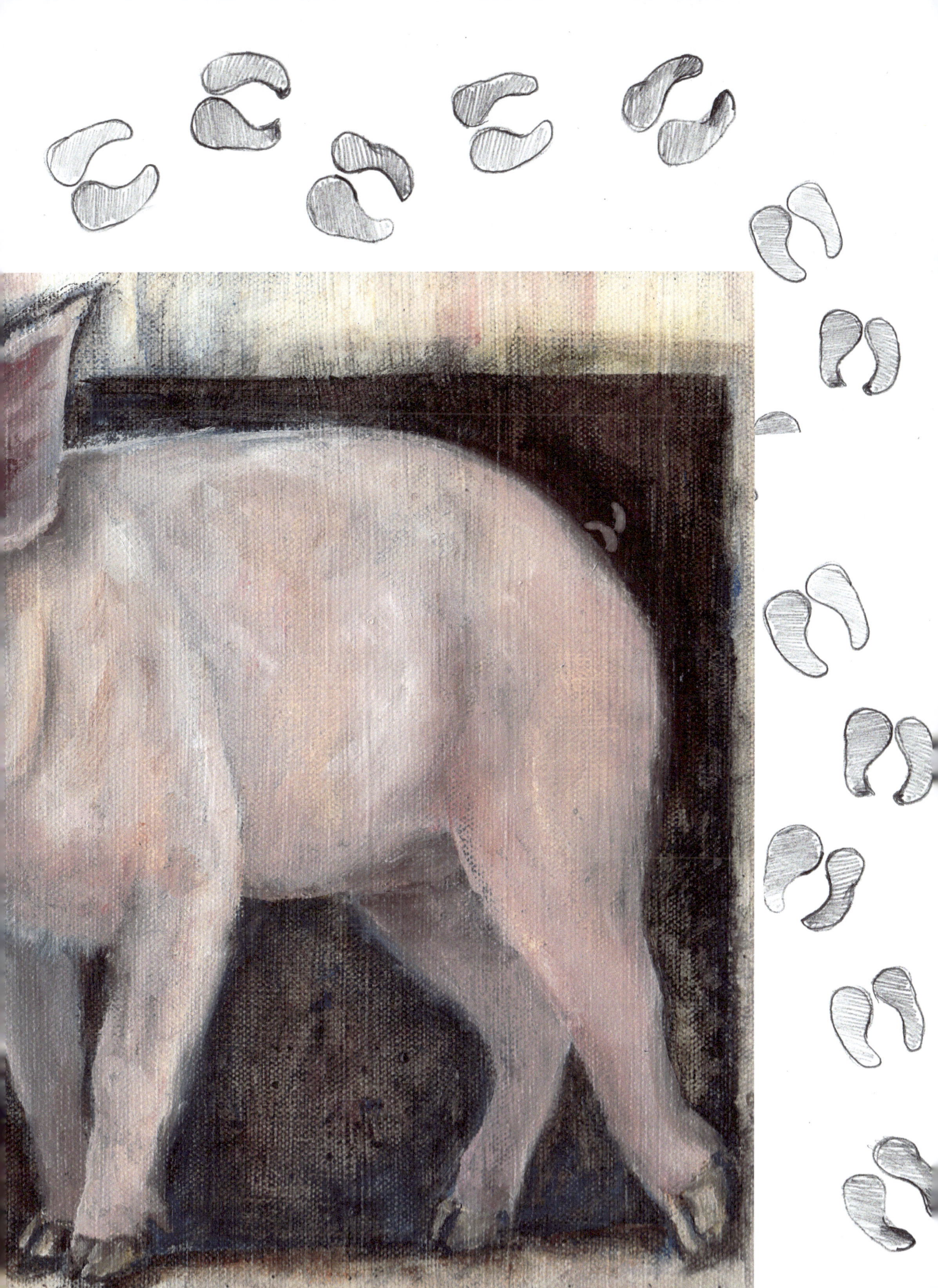

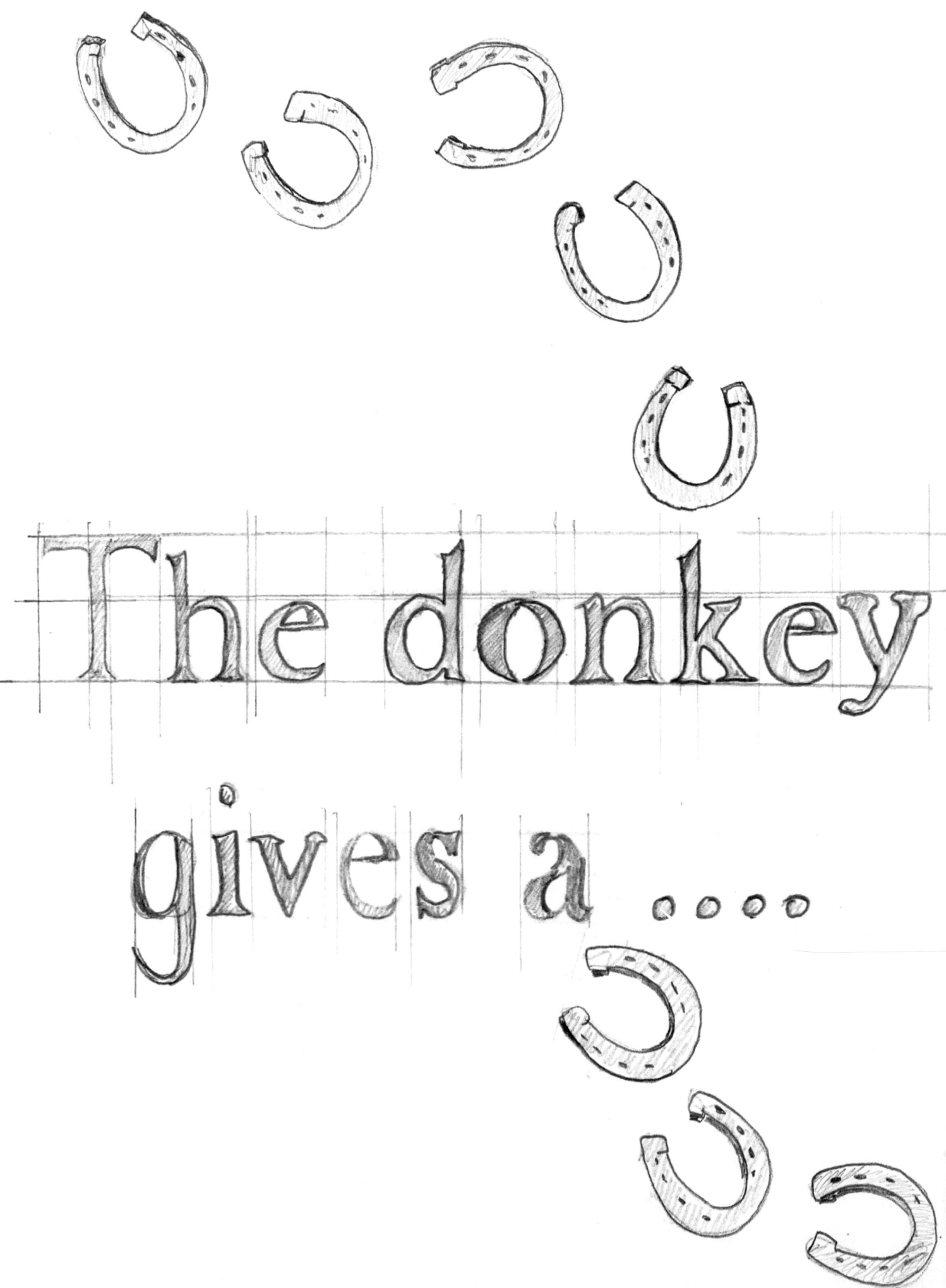

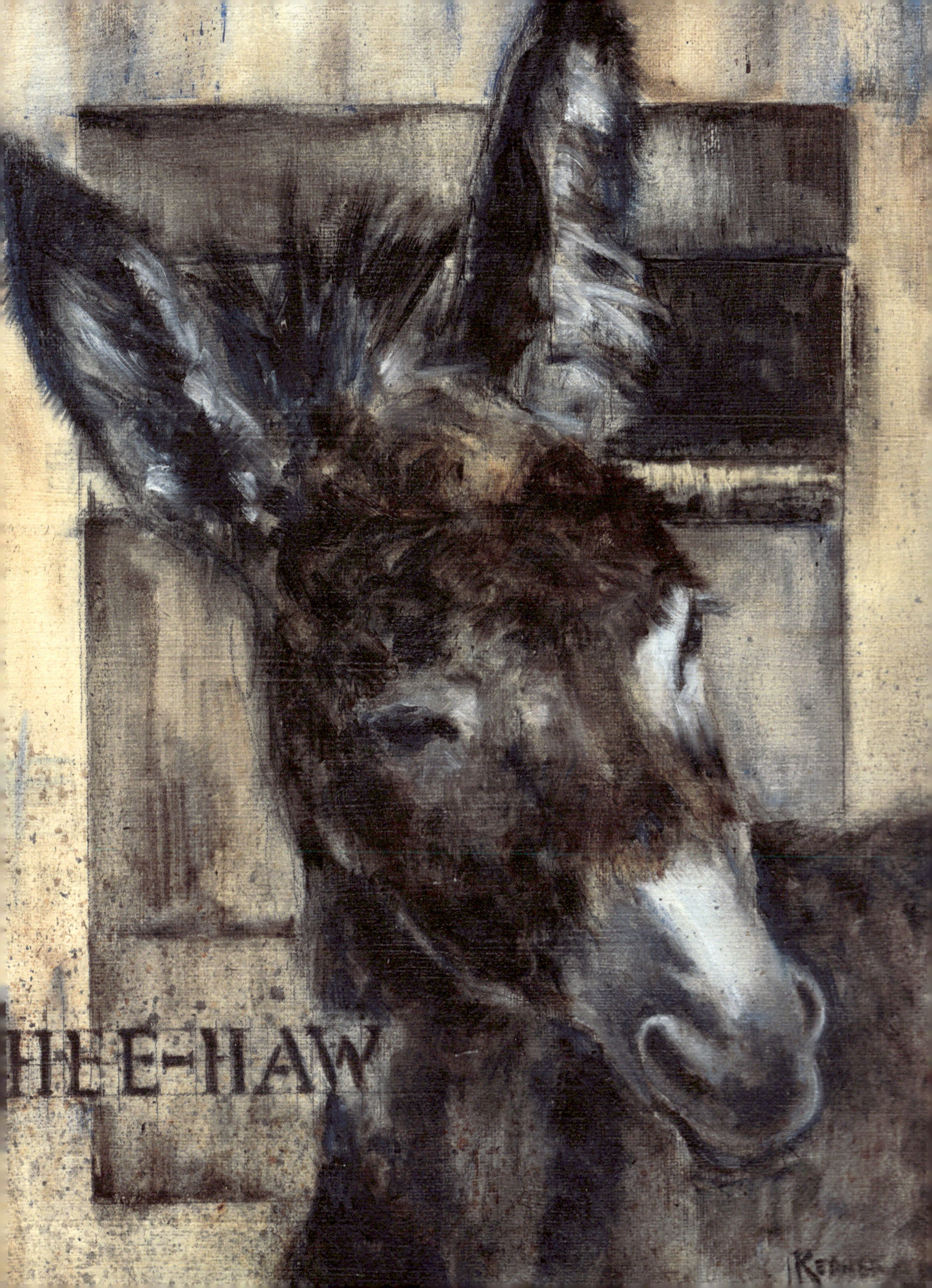

The goose gives a...

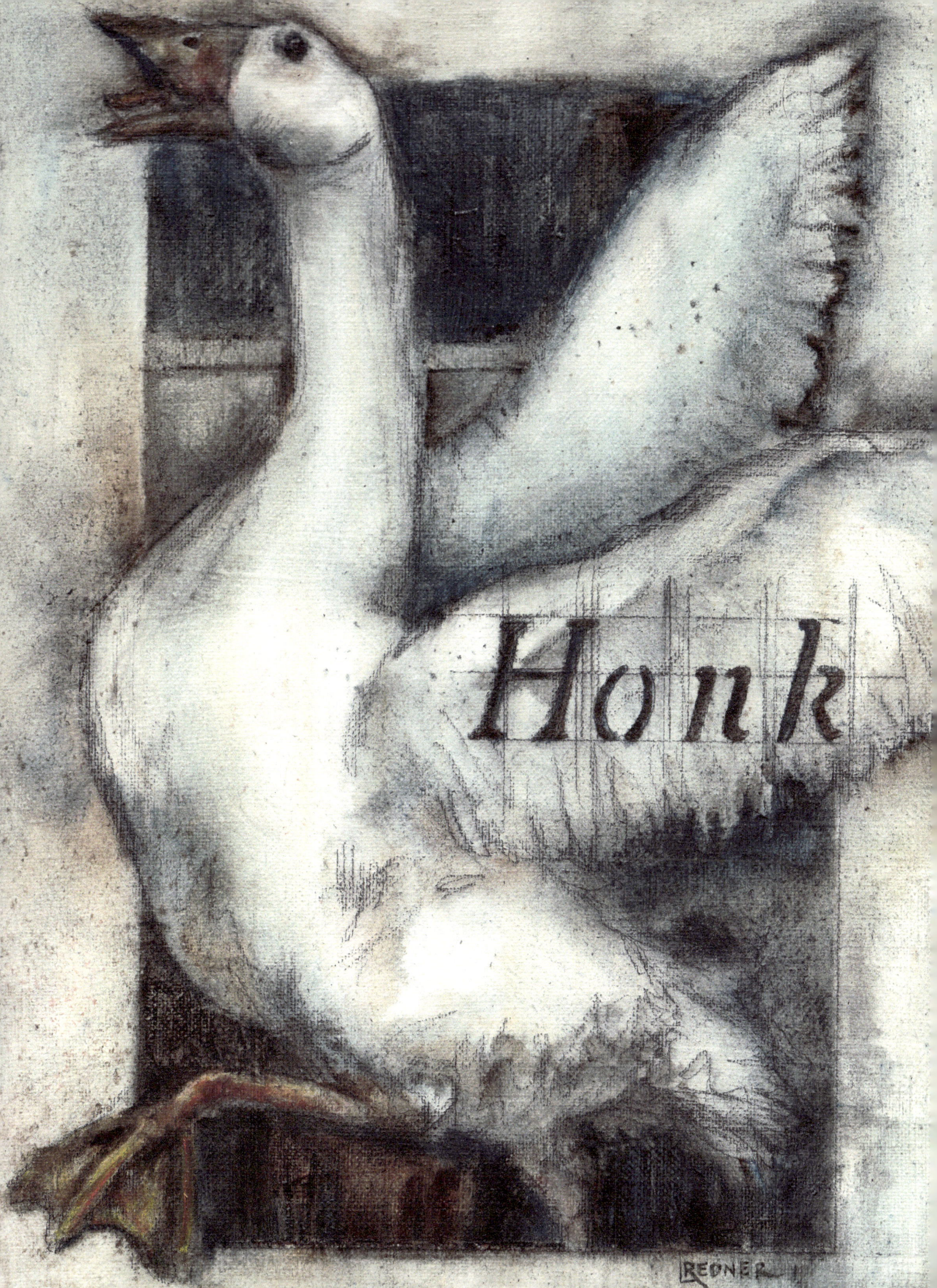

The sheep says...

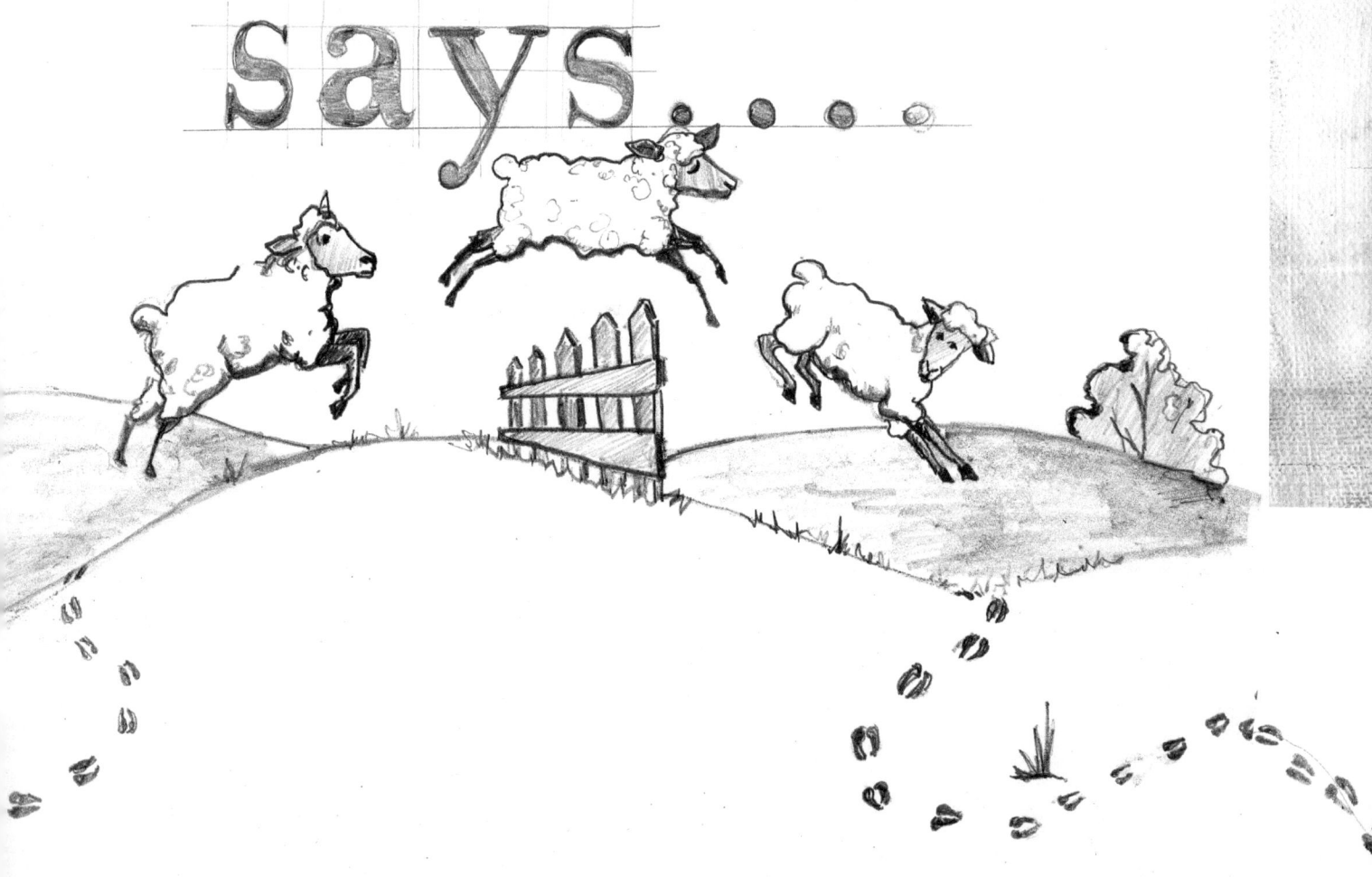

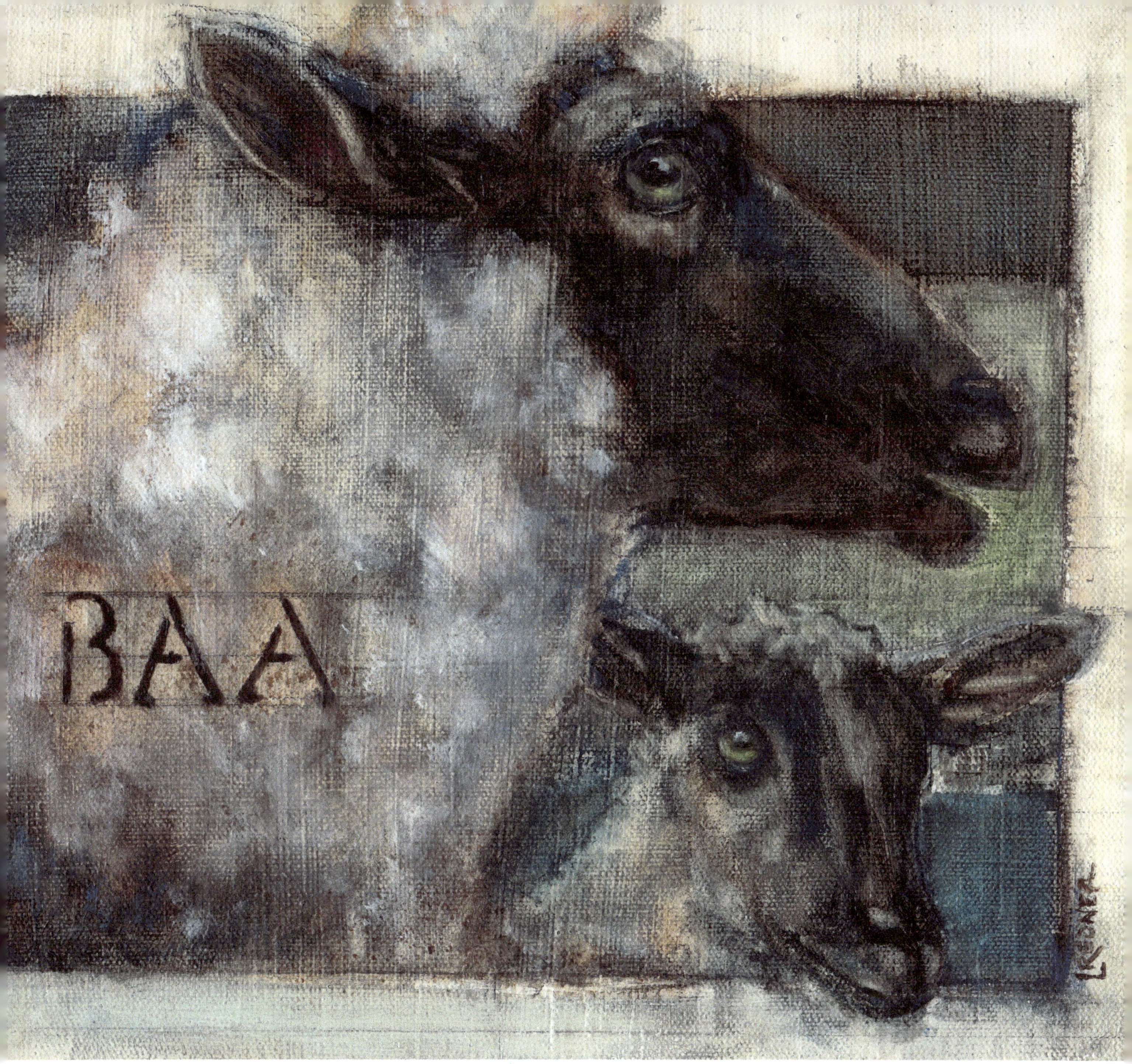

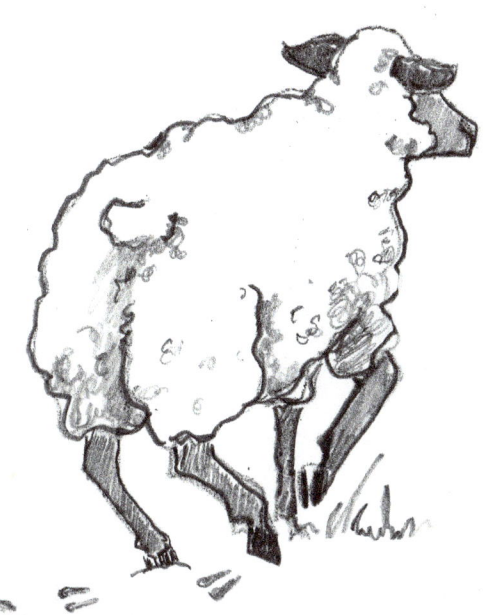
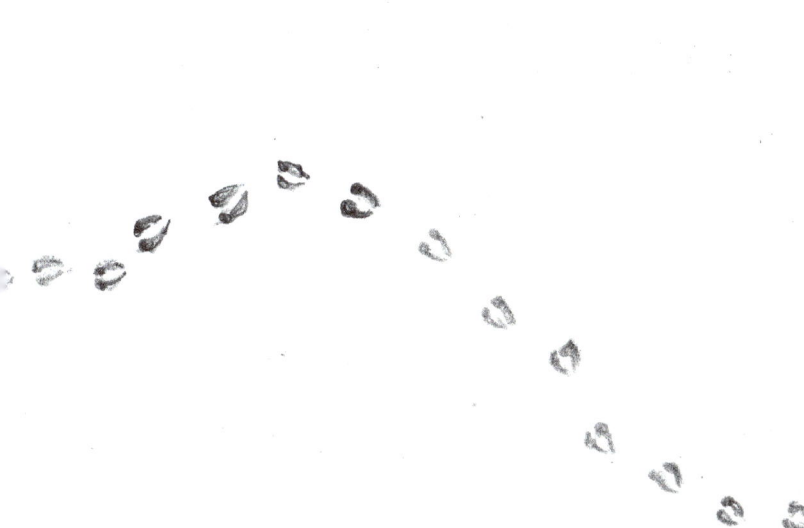

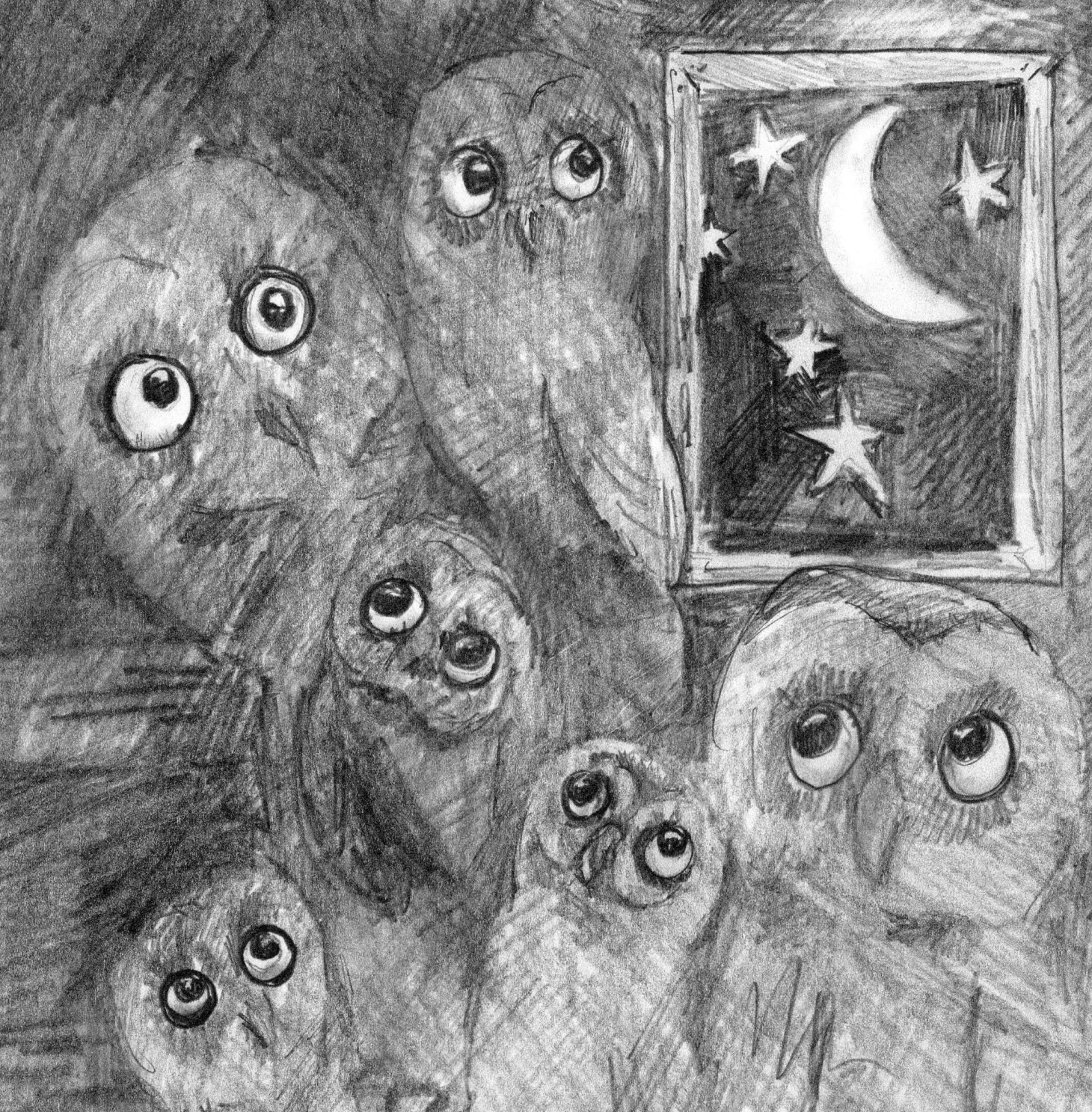

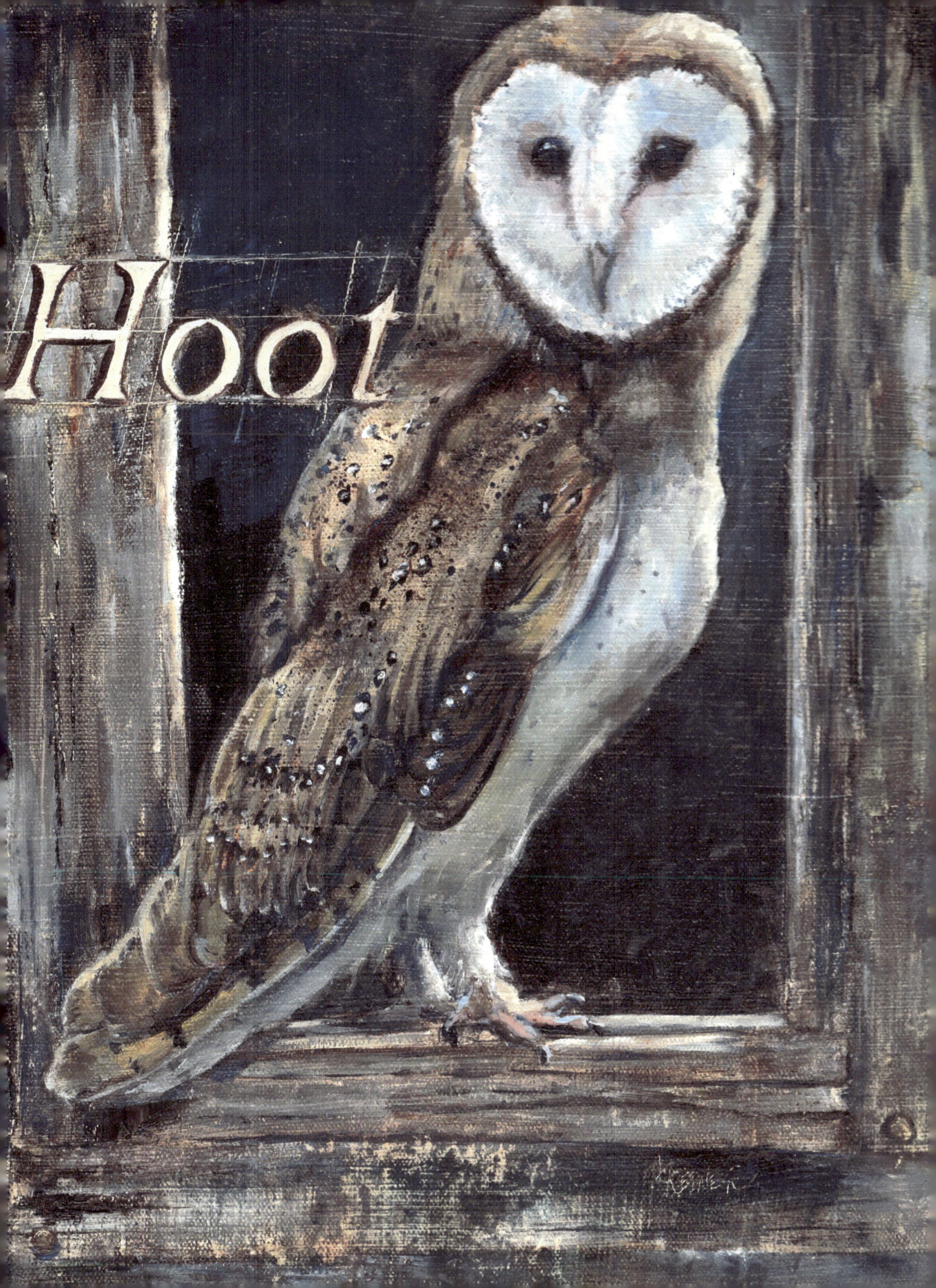

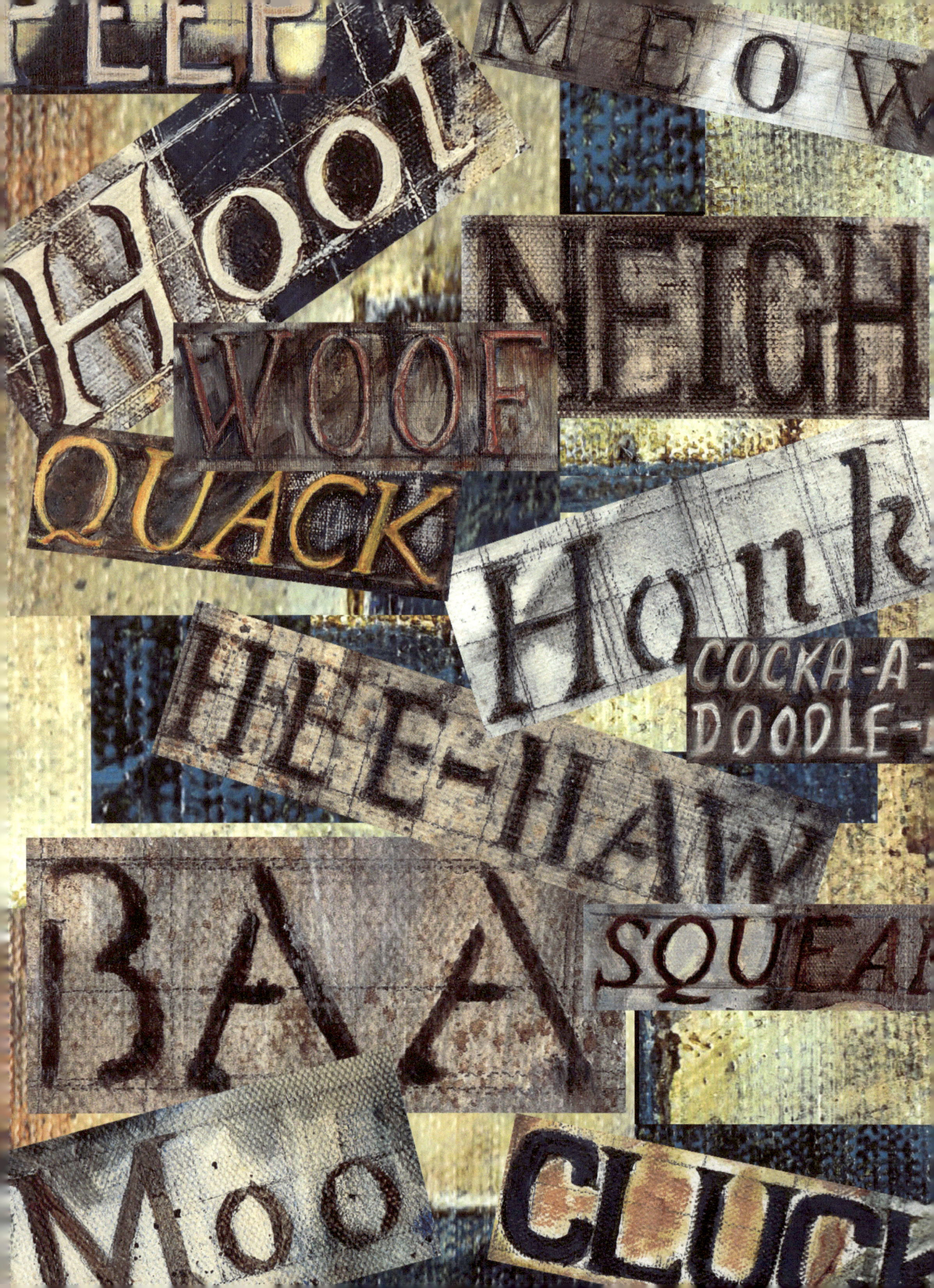

www.ingramcontent.com/pod-product-compliance
Lightning Source LLC
Chambersburg PA
CBHW051823210526
45473CB00005B/1712

9798387702976